SEA

CASPIAN SEA

Haran

River Tigris

Nineveh

A s s y r i a

River Euphrates

M e s o p o t a m i a

River Tigris

Babylon

River Euphrates

PERSIAN GULF

Sidon
Tyre
Damascus

Ramoth-Gilead

Jezreel
River Jordan
Ammon
Canaan
Jerusalem
Hebron
Beersheba
Moab
Edom
Negeb Desert

Wilderness of Paran

Midian

Mount Sinai

RED SEA

The Lands of the Old Testament

Km | 0   100   200   300   400
Miles | 0   50   100   150   200   250

The Bible
for Children

The Bible
for Children

Retold by
BRIDGET HADAWAY and JEAN ATCHESON
Foreword by
His Grace the ARCHBISHOP of CANTERBURY

Cathay Books

Acknowledgments

I would like to acknowledge my debt to the Reverend Cecil Booth for placing his library at my disposal. With his help I have been able to include many details of life at the time of Christ that were taken for granted, and therefore not mentioned, by the first writers of the New Testament.

I would also like to thank Jennifer Huggins, librarian at the King's Lynn Borough Library, for cheerfully meeting all my requests for old and new texts of the Bible.

I am deeply grateful to Alison Cathie, whose own high standard of editing has encouraged everyone concerned with the preparation of this book to give of their best.

Finally, I would like to thank my own sons and daughter for showing me the simple understanding that children have of great truth. I hope that children everywhere may share with them the enjoyment of this book.

BRIDGET HADAWAY

Norfolk

I am deeply grateful to Bridget Hadaway and to Alison Cathie for their patience and enthusiasm, without which this complicated project could never have been completed. I owe many thanks also to my three children, who patiently bore my many long absences from them in order to work on it.

For me, the most enthralling part of the work has been the chance to retell these astonishingly touching, memorable stories in a way that brings them within the scope of a modern child's own emotions and experience. I hope we have succeeded, and to whatever extent we have, the chief debt of gratitude must go to the Bible itself for preserving such a rich heritage of material.

JEAN ATCHESON

Cambridge

First published by Octopus Books Limited
This edition published by Cathay Books
59 Grosvenor Street
London W1

Reprinted 1983

© 1973 Octopus Books Limited

ISBN 0 86178 073 6

Printed in Czechoslovakia
50327/9

Foreword

By
His Grace
The Archbishop of Canterbury

I am happy to commend this book. It is a fine piece of work – not indeed a new translation but an attempt to present large parts of the Bible in such a way that children of, say, seven years of age and upwards will be able to understand it without great difficulty. Mothers of children have had a big share in the work, and their ability to enter into a child's way of thinking has proved invaluable. The pictures, which are singularly beautiful, will provide the reader with endless pleasure and profit.

Donald Cantuar:

The Old Testament

CONTENTS

The Creation	10
The Garden of Eden and the Serpent	12
Cain and Abel	14
The Flood	16
The Tower of Babel	19
The Promise to Abram	20
Abram and Lot	22
Lot's Wife	23
Abram's Vision	24
Isaac and Rebecca	26
Jacob and Esau	29
Jacob's Ladder	32
Jacob and Rachel	34
Jacob and Esau Become Friends Again	36
Joseph and His Brothers	38
Joseph in Potiphar's House	41
Pharaoh's Dreams	44
Joseph's Brothers in Egypt	47
Jacob Goes to Egypt	50
The Famine	52
The Birth of Moses	54
Moses in Midian	56

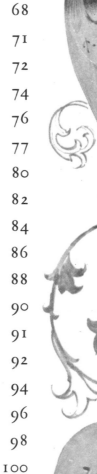

The Voice from the Burning Bush   58

Pharaoh and the Israelites   60

The Plagues of Egypt   62

The Institution of the Passover   64

The Night of the Passover   66

The Crossing of the Red Sea   68

The Israelites Find Food   71

The Water from the Rock   72

The Defeat of the Amalekites   74

Jethro Advises Moses   76

The Ten Commandments   77

The Ark of the Covenant   80

The Making of the Golden Calf   82

The Renewed Promise   84

The Departure from Sinai   86

The Twelve Spies   88

The King of Edom   90

King Balek and Balaam, the Holy Man   91

Balaam and the Angel   92

The Death of Moses   94

The Entry into Canaan   96

The Fall of Jericho   98

Joshua Conquers Canaan   100

Gideon Defeats the Midianites   103

Jotham and Abimelech	106
Jephthah's Vow	108
The Story of Samson	110
Ruth and Naomi	114
Ruth and Boaz	116
Samuel, Child of the Lord	118
Samuel and Saul	120
Saul Is Chosen King	122
Jonathan Breaks an Oath	123
Saul Disobeys God	124
David, Son of Jesse	125
David and Goliath	127
Saul's Jealousy	130
David Marries Saul's Daughter	132
David and Jonathan	134
David and Abigail	136
David the King	137
David and Bathsheba	139
David and Absalom	141
The Death of David	143
Solomon Becomes King	144
The Judgment of Solomon	145
The Building of the Temple	148
The Visit of the Queen of Sheba	150

The Ravens Feed Elijah	153
The Priests of Baal	154
The Still, Small Voice	156
Naboth's Vineyard	157
The Parting of Elijah and Elisha	158
Elisha Cures Naaman	160
The Anointing of Jehu	162
The Reign of Joash	164
The Death of Elisha	165
Josiah and Isaiah's Prophecies	167
The Fall and Destruction of Jerusalem	168
The Jewish Prisoners in Babylon	170
The King's Dream	172
The Golden Statue	173
Shadrach, Meshach and Abed-nego	175
The Interpretation and Fulfilment of the Dream	178
The Writing on the Wall	180
Daniel in the Lions' Den	182
Rebuilding the Temple	185
The Rebuilding of the Wall	186
The Story of Esther	188
God's Testing of Job	190
Jonah and the Whale	191

The Creation

BEFORE you or I were made, or the continents and seas, or the earth or the stars or the universe or space itself, God thought he would create the world. First he made the heavens and the earth, a mass of whirling clouds and vapours, without form or solidity. And everything was dark.

God saw that he had hardly begun. He said, "Let there be light," and there was light and God divided the light from the darkness and made day and night.

But there was no shape to anything that he had made so God divided the sky from the earth, and put one on top of the other.

On earth God gathered all the waters together to make the seas. He made the dry land and made grass grow on the land. He made plants that give seeds, and trees that give fruit. And when he saw what he had made, he liked it.

To mark the seasons, the days and the years, God made the sun and the moon and stars to shine in the sky, and God was pleased with these.

Then God made creatures to live on the earth. He made great whales, and the smaller fish, and every creature that moves in the sea, and he made the birds. He was glad that he had made them, and he blessed them and said, "Have children, and fill the sea and the air."

He also made all the other countless creatures that live on the earth—wild beasts and insects and things that crawl in the soil. And he liked what he had made.

Finally God said, "I will make man. I will make him in my own shape and I will give him power over all the creatures I have made." So God made man and woman. He blessed them and told them to have children, to live on the earth and to rule over it.

God said, "I have given you plants to eat. And I have given plants for the cattle and for the other beasts, and for every living creature that moves on the earth."

Then God looked at everything that he had made; and it pleased him.

In six days God had made the heavens and the earth and all its plants and creatures. His work was finished.

So on the seventh day, God rested. He blessed the seventh day, and made it a holy day for ever.

The Garden of Eden and the Serpent

WHEN the first rains had watered the earth, God made man. He took clay and moulded it into his own shape. Then he breathed life into the clay, and gave man a living soul. This first man was called Adam. God gave him a beautiful garden to live in, called the Garden of Eden, in which God had planted flowers and fruit trees of every kind. God told Adam that he could eat the fruit of every tree in the garden except one, the tree of the knowledge of good and evil. "Eat from that tree," God said to Adam, "and you will surely die."

Adam was content with his life in the garden, but God saw that of all the creatures he had made, only man had no partner. So God put Adam into a deep sleep, and while he was sleeping, God took a rib from Adam's side. From this rib God made a woman, whose name was Eve, to be a wife and a companion to Adam.

Adam and Eve lived happily in the garden. But there was one creature in the garden who wished to make trouble between God and man. This was the serpent, who was the most cunning of all the creatures God had made. One day the serpent found Eve alone in the garden, and he whispered in her ear, "You will not die if you eat the fruit of the tree of knowledge of good and evil. You will understand everything, and you will both be like gods."

Eve believed the serpent, and wanted to be a god. She took the fruit and ate it, and gave it to Adam, and he ate it too. At once everything changed. They felt guilty and unhappy for the first time. Also, they were ashamed of their nakedness, so they sewed fig leaves together to cover themselves up.

That evening, Adam and Eve heard God walking in the garden, and they hid them-

selves among the trees. "Where are you?" God called out to Adam. Then Adam had to come out of hiding. "I heard your voice," he said to God, "and I was afraid because I was naked, so I hid myself."

"Who told you that you were naked?" God asked him. "Have you eaten the fruit of the forbidden tree?" "The woman made me do it," Adam said.

"Why did you do it?" God asked Eve. "The serpent made me do it," she replied.

God grew very angry and put a curse on the serpent. Then he turned to Adam and Eve. "Because you have disobeyed me," he said, "I will send you out of the Garden of Eden into the wilderness, where life will be hard for you. Woman will give birth in pain, and man will have to work hard to raise crops, until he dies. I made you out of dust, and you will return to dust."

So Adam and Eve had to leave the garden where they had been so happy, and God set an angel to guard it with a flaming sword so that they could never return.

Cain and Abel

LIFE was hard for Adam and Eve outside the garden, as God had said it would be. Eve gave birth to a son, whom she called Cain. Soon afterwards, she had another baby whom she named Abel. Now she and Adam had two sons to help them grow their crops and take care of their animals. When the boys grew up Cain became a farmer and worked in the fields, raising crops, while Abel became a shepherd and looked after the sheep.

Adam and Eve used to show their love and respect for God by offering sacrifices to him. They would build an altar out of stones, light a fire, and then kill the finest young lamb or goat in their flock by cutting its throat and pouring the blood into a bowl. Then they would burn its body in the fire. They brought other offerings too—fruit, vegetables and grain, but always the gift they sacrificed was the best of its kind, to say Thank you to God, who had provided it.

One day, Cain and Abel made sacrifices too. Cain brought grain from his harvest and Abel brought young lambs from his flock. God was pleased with Abel's sacrifice because he had offered it gladly; but he knew that Cain had not really wanted to make his offering, so he did not accept it. This made Cain very angry. "Why are you cross?" God said to Cain. "If you do well and give gladly, your offering will be accepted, but if your thoughts are full of evil, then evil will rule you."

Then Cain was not only angry but jealous of Abel, and when they were next out in the fields together he beat him so badly that he killed him.

When Cain came home, God said to him, "Where is your brother Abel?" and Cain replied, "I don't know—it's not my job to know where he is."

"What have you done?" God said to Cain. "I know you have killed your brother—his blood is crying out to me from the earth. From now on you will never again be able to farm, or bring in the harvest. You must wander like a stranger for the rest of your days, and never belong anywhere."

"That means I will never see you again and never have a home again, and everyone who finds me will want to kill me," Cain pleaded with God. "I don't think I can bear such a dreadful punishment."

God marked Cain with a special mark so that men would know he had killed his brother and no one would kill him, and this meant he had to undergo the punishment of living without friends for the rest of his life.

The Flood

YEARS passed, and many people lived on the earth, but they had become very wicked. They argued and fought and stole and lied, and cheated one another so badly that God became sorry that he had made people who were causing such trouble and he decided he would destroy them all.

But there was among them one man who was good. His name was Noah, and God loved him. So he spoke to Noah and told him what he was going to do. He would send so much rain that there would be a great flood, and it would drown everything on the earth.

When Noah heard this he was very frightened, but God said, "Don't worry, Noah, you are a good man, and I won't destroy you or your wife, or your sons, or

their wives. But you must do exactly as I tell you, so that when the flood comes you will be saved."

God told Noah to build a great boat called an ark. It was to be 450 feet long, 75 feet wide and 45 feet high. It was to be made of cypress wood, covered with reeds and coated with tar both inside and out. Noah cut and sawed, and bent and shaped. He built three decks, cut a large door in one side and put a window in the top.

The people who lived nearby laughed at Noah while he was building the ark. "Why build a boat here—we're nowhere near the sea. You must be mad," they said.

But Noah paid no attention.

"This big ark is not only for you," God said to Noah. "I want you to go out and collect a male and a female of every kind of animal and bird and reptile, and take them into the ark with you. Now go and gather all the food you can find for you and for them. You will need enough for a long voyage."

When Noah's neighbours saw Noah and his family piling stores of fruit and grain, leaves and hay, inside the ark, they jeered louder than ever. But Noah and his family paid no attention and went on with their work. Two of every kind of animal and bird and reptile eat a lot of food, and very soon it would begin to rain.

When all the stores were ready, Noah and his wife and his sons and his sons' wives went out to collect the animals. They followed Noah into the ark, two by two. As soon as every one of them was safely on board, the first drops of rain started to fall.

It rained and it rained. Quite soon the ark began to float, but the water rose and rose, until it covered even the mountaintops and every living creature that was not on the ark was drowned. But it still rained. It rained for 40 days and 40 nights, and after it had finally stopped raining, the flood waters went on covering the whole earth for 150 days.

Then God thought of Noah and the ark, and he made a strong wind blow, and the flood waters gradually went down. At last the ark came to rest on the top of a mountain. Noah began to send out birds, to see if they could find dry land, but they could find no place to perch. Finally one day Noah sent out a dove, and that evening the dove came back with an olive twig in its beak. Some parts of the land were dry again. The next time Noah released the dove, it did not come back at all, which showed Noah that it was now safe to leave the ark.

So Noah and his family, and all the creatures they had taken with them, came out of the ark onto dry land, and Noah built an altar and offered a sacrifice of thanksgiving. God was pleased, and he blessed Noah and his family and told them to have many children and fill the earth with people again.

"I will make a promise to you and all your children," God said. "I will never again send a flood to destroy everything. I will put a rainbow in every rain cloud, and whenever you see it you can remember my promise, which will last for ever."

The Tower
of Babel

The Tower of Babel

THERE was once a time when everyone spoke the same language and understood one another perfectly. In those days the people of the earth wandered westwards, looking for a place to settle.

When they came to a plain in the land of Shinar, they said, "How beautiful a city would look here in place of this wilderness! Instead of trees and grass we will have houses and avenues. We will build a great wall around the city, to protect us. We will make domes that gleam in the sun, and gardens and fountains to cool us after our work. We will sink wells deep into the earth and build towers that reach into the sky. We will begin by building a tower that will be so high that it will reach to God himself."

After a while God came to look at their city and their tower, and was very angry. "If men can do this," he said to himself, "there is nothing they won't be able to do. I will confuse their speech, and make them all speak different languages, so that they won't be able to understand one another."

Suddenly, not one person could understand what anybody else was saying. There was terrible confusion in the city. All the work stopped, and the people went off in different directions and scattered themselves over the face of the earth.

The city, which was left unfinished, was given the name of Babel, because it was the place where God had made a babble out of the inhabitants' speech.

The Promise to Abram

THERE was once a man called Abram, who lived in the city of Haran, in Mesopotamia. Abram was a good man, and he loved his wife Sarai, but they had never had any children. One day God said to Abram, "You must leave your house, and your relations, and your country –I am going to show you a new country. I have chosen you to be the father of a great new nation, and I will bless you and make your name so famous that men will always remember it. I will bless everyone who blesses you, and curse anyone who curses you. All the families on earth will pray to be blessed as you are blessed."

Abram did as God had commanded him, and set out from Haran, taking his wife Sarai, his nephew Lot, and his flocks, his money and his servants. They journeyed until they reached the land of Canaan, where the Canaanites were living. There God appeared to Abram again, and said, "I give this land to you and to your family for ever." Abram built an altar at the spot where he had heard God's voice, and offered a sacrifice. Then he travelled on, towards the Negeb desert.

There was a great famine in the land of Canaan, so Abram took his family to Egypt, to live for a while in the land that was ruled by the Pharaohs. On the way there Abram said to Sarai, "You are so beautiful that I am afraid the Egyptians will kill me so that they can make you one of Pharaoh's wives. Let's say that you are my sister, not my wife, and then they will treat me well so as to gain favour with you." So they agreed on this plan.

When they arrived in Egypt, just as Abram had expected, Pharaoh's courtiers admired Sarai's beauty and told their king that he should take her as his wife. Then Pharaoh sent Abram many gifts, sheep and cattle and donkeys and camels, and slaves, both male and female, and he took Sarai into his household with the intention of making her one of his wives.

But God at once made Pharaoh and all his household fall ill with a great sickness. Pharaoh realized that Abram's God was doing this to him on account of Sarai, and he called Abram to him and said: "Why did you let me make this dreadful mistake? You should have told me she was your wife. Now take her and go away."

So Abram left Egypt and went back to the Negeb with Sarai and his nephew Lot, and all the silver and gold and cattle in their possession. He was now a wealthy man, for Pharaoh had been generous with his gifts, and had not insisted that Abram give them back before he left Egypt.

God said to Abram, "Look up, and look far into the distance, north and south and east and west. I will give the land as far as you can see to you and to your descendants for ever. I will make them as countless as the grains of dust on the ground. Now go and explore the land, for it is rightfully yours."

Then Abram travelled the length and breadth of the land God had given him, and built an altar to God in the plains of Hebron.

Abram and Lot

WHEN Abram first returned to Canaan with his nephew Lot he found that the land was too poor to provide enough food and water for the families and servants and cattle of both Lot and himself. Quarrels broke out between Abram's herdsmen and Lot's herdsmen. Then Abram said to Lot, "You and I should not quarrel, and nor should our servants. There is open country ahead of us. Why don't we part company? If you go to the left, I will go right; if you go right, I will go to the left. You choose which way you want to go."

Lot looked around him and saw how well watered the plain around the river Jordan was. It was as green as the plains around the river Nile in Egypt. So Lot chose the plain of Jordan as the place he would like to live, and he settled near the city of Sodom.

Some time later the kings of five neighbouring kingdoms went to war against four other kings of the plain of Jordan, two of whom were the kings of Sodom and its twin city, Gomorrah. The four kings were defeated and Lot and his family were taken prisoner along with their leaders.

When Abram heard that his nephew had been captured, he called all his men together and they pursued the enemy and surrounded them by night. Abram rescued Lot and all the other captives, and was blessed by the high priest for his goodness and bravery.

Lot's Wife

Now the people who lived in the cities of Sodom and Gomorrah were known far and wide for the disgusting lives they led. But before God in his anger destroyed the two cities, he sent two messengers to Sodom to see whether there were any good men still living there. For he would have spared all the others if there had been even five men worth saving.

The messengers arrived in Sodom in the evening, and found Lot sitting near the city gate. He welcomed them, and invited them to eat with him and to sleep at his house.

While they were eating, the men of Sodom came and beat on Lot's door.

"Bring out those strangers," they cried. "We want to have our fun with them."

"No," Lot shouted back, "these men are my guests."

"Then we'll kill you instead," cried the men, and they tried to break down the door to get at Lot. But God struck every one of them blind where they stood so they could not find the door.

"Flee for your life," God's messengers said to Lot, "and take your wife and your daughters with you. These people must be punished, but don't look back and don't stop, or you will be swept away like them."

Then God made a storm like an erupting volcano, and fire and ashes rained down onto Sodom and Gomorrah, and earthquakes shook the cities to the ground. Everything was destroyed, except Lot fleeing with his wife and daughters.

But Lot's wife stopped and looked back, reluctant to leave the pleasures of the city — and she was turned into a pillar of salt.

Abram's Vision

WHEN Abram was an old man God appeared to him in a vision and said, "Don't be afraid, Abram, for I am going to give you great rewards. Look at the stars in the sky. You will have as many descendants as there are stars."

"But, Lord," said Abram, "Sarai and I have never had a child, and now we are too old to have one."

"Trust me," God said to him, "and I will make you a promise. For a time your family will live in a foreign land and men will be cruel to them. But I will punish the nation that makes them into slaves, and send them home again as wealthy men. I give this land of Canaan, from the Nile to the Euphrates river, to you and to your descendants for all time. Your name will no longer be Abram but Abraham, for you will be the father of many nations. Your part of the promise is that you will have every male child born in your household circumcized. I will not accept an uncircumcized man as a member of your family."

Then God said, "As for Sarai, your wife, she too will have a new name, Sarah. Old as she is, I will bless her so that she will give you a son, and you must call him Isaac. Ishmael, the son you have had by your slave woman Hagar, will be the father of princes and of a great nation. But it is Isaac, the

son you and Sarah will have, whose children will fulfil the promise I have made."

Abraham and Sarah waited quietly for God's promise to be fulfilled. One day three men appeared at their tent, and Abraham gave them food to eat and water to refresh themselves. "Your son will be born in the spring," said the men, who were messengers from God.

Spring came, and Sarah gave birth to a son. They called him Isaac, and Abraham circumcized him.

When Isaac had grown into a boy God decided to test Abraham's faith. He ordered him to take his son into the mountains and kill him, instead of the lamb he usually killed, as a sacrifice to God.

Abraham loved Isaac dearly, but he also loved God. He set off for the mountains with a very heavy heart, and Isaac came with him, carrying the wood for the fire. When they came to the hills Isaac said to his father, "Father, we've come all this way, but we didn't bring a young lamb to kill in God's honour." "God will provide the sacrifice," said Abraham.

When they came to the right place, Abraham built an altar out of stones and lit a fire on it. Then he tied Isaac up, and was just about to raise his knife to kill the terrified boy when God called to him to stop.

"There is a ram nearby which has caught its horns in a bush. Offer that as a sacrifice instead of your beloved son. Now I know beyond any doubt the extent of your faith and love for me."

Abraham untied Isaac and held him close to him. They caught the ram and sacrificed it as God had told them to. Then the father and son went home together, rejoicing.

[25]

Isaac and Rebecca

WHEN Abraham was very old, he wanted his son Isaac to find a wife. But he did not want him to marry a woman from Canaan, where God had sent them to live; only one from his own country, from Haran, far to the north, would do. So Abraham called an old and trusted servant to him and said:

"Go to the land of my fathers. I want you to find a wife there for Isaac, from among my own family."

The servant said, "But what if the girl does not want to come back with me to a strange land? Wouldn't it be better if your son made the journey to your own country himself?"

Abraham replied, "No, Isaac must not leave this place. God commanded us to settle here, and God will guide you on your way and show you which is the woman who will become my son's wife."

So the servant set out on the journey with ten camels and many gifts. It was evening when he at last came to the city of Haran. He was tired after his long journey so he made his camels kneel down by the well while he waited for the women of the city to come there to draw water. He prayed to God to give him a sign so that he would know which of them ought to be Isaac's bride.

Before he had quite finished his prayer, a beautiful young girl named Rebecca, who was the daughter of Abraham's brother Bethuel, came walking towards him carrying a water pitcher on her shoulder. When she had carefully filled the pitcher with water Abraham's servant asked her for a sip of it. Willingly, she offered it to the old

man. Then she said, "Your camels must be thirsty too. I will draw them as much water as they need."

The servant took a golden ring and two heavy gold bracelets out of his saddle bag and gave them to Rebecca. "Please tell me whose daughter you are," he said, "and whether you think your father can give me shelter for the night?" "My father's name is Bethuel," she replied, "and I'm sure we have plenty of room for you and your animals." She ran ahead of him to the house, and as soon as her brother Laban saw the golden jewellery she was wearing, he hastened outside to welcome the tired traveller. The old man was given water to wash himself, and food to eat, and fodder was brought for his camels. But he would not sit down to eat until he had told Rebecca's family why he was there:

"Since my master Abraham left this city he has been greatly blessed by God, and has become powerful and rich. He has flocks of sheep and herds of cattle, he has silver and gold, slaves, camels and donkeys. My master's son Isaac will inherit all this wealth, and my master wants him to marry a wife from among his own family here in Haran. When I came to this city and rested by the well outside the gate, I prayed, 'Oh God, when the first young woman comes from the city to draw water, I will say to her, "Please give me some water to drink." If she then offers me water and my camels too, I shall take that as a sign that she is meant to be the bride.'

"Before I had even finished praying I saw Rebecca coming out with her pitcher on her shoulder. Then everything happened

just as I had prayed to God that it should. She offered me the water, and she gave water to my camels, and she told me she was one of Abraham's own family. Then I gave her gifts and she led me to you. Now tell me if you will let her come back with me to be Isaac's bride."

Rebecca's father, Bethuel, and her brother Laban could not doubt that God wanted her to go, so they called Rebecca and asked her if she was prepared to leave her home and go with Abraham's servant that very day. "Yes, I am," she said, and she and her nurse packed their saddle bags, mounted their camels and rode away with the old man.

Isaac was walking by himself in the fields one evening a few days later when he looked up and saw the travellers coming towards him. Rebecca saw him too, and asked the servant who he was. "It is my master," the old man replied, and she quickly jumped down from her camel. Isaac came to meet her, and took her to his mother's tent.

Abraham thanked the old servant for doing his work so well and bringing back such a lovely bride. And Rebecca and Isaac were married, and loved each other dearly.

Jacob and Esau

ISAAC and Rebecca had been married for years, but they were sad because they had not had any children. Then Isaac prayed to God to give them a child, and God listened to Isaac and answered his prayers. Rebecca gave birth to twin boys. Before they were born God said to Rebecca, "Your sons will be the fathers of two nations. One will be stronger than the other and the older will be the servant of the younger."

The boys were born and their parents called them Esau and Jacob. Esau, the elder, became a hunter and roamed the plains in search of deer. Jacob preferred to stay at home among his father's tents. Isaac's favourite was Esau, but Rebecca favoured Jacob.

One day Esau returned from hunting ravenously hungry and impatient to eat. "Let me have some of that bread and soup you have made," he said to Jacob. "Not until you have sold me your right as first-born son to inherit most of what our father owns," Jacob replied.

Esau barely took time to think over Jacob's demand. His birthright seemed nothing in comparison with his need for a hearty meal at once. "I'm nearly dead with hunger and exhaustion—what use is my birthright to me now?" he thought. So he swore an oath and gave his birthright to Jacob in exchange for the food his brother had cooked.

Time went by and Isaac became nearly blind. One day he called Esau to him and said: "I am old and my life will soon be over. Take your bow and arrows and shoot me a deer on the plains. Cook the meat the way I like it, and then bring it to me to eat, and I will give you a special blessing."

Rebecca had overheard Isaac's words and as soon as Esau had set off for the hunt she said to Jacob, "Now listen to me, and do exactly as I say. Pick out two young kids from our herd of goats. I will cook them the way your father likes, in a sauce made with bitter herbs, and then you can take them to him and say you are Esau. Then he will give you the special blessing that a father gives the son who will be his heir."

"But Esau is hairy," Jacob said, "and my skin is smooth. I know my father can't see well, but as soon as he touches me he will know that I am trying to trick him, and he will curse me instead of blessing me." "Don't worry," said his mother, "just bring me the kids."

So Jacob killed two kids and Rebecca skinned them and cooked them with herbs. She covered Jacob's arms and neck with the skins and dressed him in some of Esau's clothes. Then she put the dish of meat into his hands, and he took it to his father and asked for his blessing.

"Come close and let me feel you, my son," said Isaac, "so that I can be sure you really are Esau." Jacob came and kneeled by his father so that Isaac could touch him with his hands. "You sound like Jacob," his father said, "but your arms feel like Esau's," and he stroked the hairy skins. "Are you

really Esau?" he asked, and Jacob lied and said he was.

Isaac ate the meat Jacob had brought and then he asked his son to kiss him. As he put his arms around Jacob, he recognized the smell of Esau on his clothes and felt certain he was embracing his first-born son, so he gave him the special blessing:

"May God always give you water and the rich harvest of the earth. People will serve you and nations will honour you. You will be the leader among your brothers, and they must do as you say. I set my curse on anyone who does harm to you and give my blessing to everyone who helps you."

Jacob had no sooner left his father than Esau came back from the hunt, carrying a deer he had killed. He cooked the meat the way his father liked it, and then he brought it to him and asked for his blessing.

"But who are you?" asked Isaac, and

Esau replied, "I am Esau, your first-born son."

Isaac began to tremble. "Who was it," he asked, "who brought me the meat just now? I ate it and blessed *him*, and that blessing must stand."

Then Esau cried out loudly and bitterly, "Bless me too, father."

"Your brother has taken the blessing," Isaac answered. "I have made him your chief and given him everything I have."

"Haven't you any blessing left for me?" cried Esau. "Please bless me too, father."

"You will always live without having much," Isaac said to him. "You will earn your living by fighting, and you will have to serve your brother. But in time you will break away and be a free man."

From then on Esau hated Jacob and planned to kill him. Esau said to himself, "My father Isaac will soon die, and then I will kill my brother, for he has cheated me and taken both my birthright and my father's special blessing."

Jacob's Ladder

REBECCA soon found out that Esau was planning to kill his brother Jacob, and she at once became very frightened. She knew Esau might make an attack on his brother at any time, and that if Jacob fought back she might then lose both of her sons.

"You must leave here at once," she told Jacob, "and you ought to go as far away as you can. My brother Laban still lives in Haran. Go to him; he will give you a home for a while. Then, when Esau's anger has died down, I will send you a message saying you can come home again."

So Jacob decided he ought to leave Beersheba as soon as he could. But his mother told his father what he intended to do, and the evening before Jacob left, Isaac sent for him and said:

"I want you to choose a wife while you are in Haran, from among our own people. I don't want you to marry a woman from the land of Canaan. God will bless you, you will have a whole nation of descendants, and this land of Canaan will be yours, just as God promised your grandfather Abraham."

So Jacob set out by himself for Haran. Although his father's blessing had made him the heir to all Isaac's flocks and herds, he carried nothing with him, except some food for the journey. His only clothes were the ones he was wearing. He walked all day and late into the evening until he was too tired to go on. So he stopped to rest. He made a pillow out of a stone that was lying nearby. Then he wrapped himself in his cloak and lay down to sleep.

He dreamed that he saw a ladder which reached from the ground right up to heaven, and that angels were moving up and down it. God seemed to be standing beside him, and he said to Jacob:

"I give the land where you are lying to you and to your descendants. They will be as countless as the dust on the earth, and will spread far and wide, north and south and east and west. I will be with you and protect you, wherever you go, and I will bring you back again to this land, to fulfil the promise I made to Abraham, your grandfather."

Then Jacob woke up, and at once he knew that he had truly been in the presence of God. He took the stone he had used as a pillow and set it up as a sacred pillar, and poured oil over it as a thanksgiving to God.

Jacob and Rachel

As JACOB travelled towards Haran, he wondered what life would be like among all the relations he did not know, and whom he would find to marry. He had almost reached the city when he saw a well with several flocks of sheep gathered around it. He asked the shepherds who were minding the sheep where they came from, and they told him they were from Haran. "Do you know my uncle Laban?" Jacob asked them. "Indeed we do," they replied, "and here comes his daughter Rachel with his flock."

When Rachel came up to the well, Jacob helped her to water her sheep. Then he told her who he was, and she at once ran home to tell her father. Laban hurried out to greet his nephew and welcomed him to his home.

So Jacob stayed with Laban and worked for him. "You shouldn't work for nothing just because you are my nephew," Laban said to him one day. "How can I repay you?" "I will work seven years for nothing," Jacob replied, "if you will give me your daughter Rachel as my wife."

Now Laban had two daughters: Leah, the elder, was plain and slow and Rachel, the younger, was graceful and beautiful. Laban said to Jacob, "You will make a good

husband. Work for me for seven years and then you can take Rachel as your wife." So Jacob worked for Laban, and the years seemed like days because he loved Rachel so much.

When his time was up, Jacob said to Laban, "I have served you well. Now give me Rachel so that we can be married and live together."

So Laban gave a great feast in honour of the wedding. But that night he brought his elder daughter to Jacob, pretending that she was Rachel. In the morning, when Jacob saw that he had married the wrong sister, he cried out, "What have you done? It was Rachel I worked for all these years, not Leah."

"In our country," Laban replied, "it is not proper for the younger daughter to be married before the elder. I will give Rachel to you as your second wife if you will work for me another seven years."

So Rachel became Jacob's wife too, and he loved her more than ever. But he still had to work another seven years for his uncle.

He worked hard and grew rich, and his wives gave him many sons. But Laban was jealous of Jacob's success and Jacob began to feel homesick. One night God appeared to him in a dream and said, "Go back to Canaan, to the land of your fathers. I will protect you."

So Jacob gathered his flocks and herds together and saddled his camels, and set off with his wives and his sons and all his possessions, to return to the land of Canaan. He did not tell Laban they were leaving because he was afraid his uncle might try to prevent him from going, or take back his daughters, Leah and Rachel. What he did not know was that Rachel had taken with her the family's household gods—the images her father used when they all worshipped together, and which he treasured beyond anything else he owned.

Jacob and Esau Become Friends Again

WHEN Laban found out that Jacob had gone, he rode after him in anger. But God told him in a dream that he must not hurt his son-in-law.

"Why did you go away without telling me?" Laban asked Jacob, when he caught up with him. "And why did you steal my household gods?"

"I was afraid you would stop me, or stop my wives from coming with me," Jacob replied. "But I did not steal your gods. Search my camp, and take back anything that is yours."

Laban searched every tent and every bag, but he did not find his gods, for Rachel had hidden them in her camel saddle and was sitting on them. So Laban and Jacob made friends, and Laban blessed his family and rode home again.

When they were about to cross the river that lay between Haran and the land of Canaan, Jacob sent messengers on ahead to tell his brother Esau of his return. When they came back, the messengers told Jacob they had met Esau, and that he was coming towards his brother with 400 men.

Jacob was afraid when he heard this, for he knew that Esau had wanted to kill him in revenge for their father's blessing which Jacob had falsely taken from him so many years before. "Oh God of my fathers," Jacob prayed now, "you commanded me to return here and promised to protect me and reward me. Protect us now, and save all my family from my brother's revenge."

Jacob decided to offer Esau a present of goats and sheep, camels and cows and donkeys—some 600 animals in all. He sent them ahead of the party in a long line and told their herdsmen to tell Esau that Jacob had sent them.

Later that evening he sent his family ahead while he himself rested by the river. At midnight, he started wading across. When he had reached the middle, a dark shape stopped him and wrestled with him,

threatening to force him below the water.
"Who are you?" Jacob gasped, but no
sound came and Jacob was forced to stand
and struggle until dawn. As the daylight
came, the thing begged Jacob to release it.
Jacob knew then that it was an angel of
darkness, and he would not let it go until it
had blessed him. Finally it said, "You shall
be blessed, Jacob, and your name shall be
Israel, for you have struggled with God and
man."

That morning Esau and his men came
near. Jacob made everybody halt while he
walked slowly forward to meet his brother,
bowing to him as he went. But Esau did not
wait for Jacob to reach him. He ran forward,
and the two brothers fell into each other's
arms, and wept with joy. Esau accepted
Jacob's gift and welcomed him back to the
land of Canaan. And from that day onwards
they became firm friends.

Joseph and His Brothers

God had commanded Jacob to return to the land of Canaan, to farm it together with his sons. Jacob had twelve sons, but only two of them were the children of his best-loved wife, Rachel. The elder of the two, named Joseph, Jacob loved more than all his other children, but he loved the younger, whose name was Benjamin, almost as much.

By the time Joseph was seventeen his brothers had come to hate him because they were jealous of their father's great love for the boy. Their anger was increased when Joseph showed them a coat Jacob had given him. It was made in many colours and had sleeves of the kind that princes wore. "Our father spoils the boy," they thought to themselves.

One night, Joseph had a dream, and in the morning he told it to his brothers. "I dreamed that we were all out in the fields, binding up the sheaves, and my sheaf rose on its end and stood upright, while your sheaves gathered round it and bowed down to the ground."

"What!" said his brothers. "Do you think that you will be king some day and rule over us?" And they hated him even more than before.

Joseph had another dream, and this he told to his father as well as his brothers. "In my dream," he said, "the sun and the moon and eleven stars were all bowing down before me."

Even his father grew angry with him then. "What is this dream of yours?" he said. "Must we all come and bow low before you, I and your mother and your brothers, just as if you were a king?"

After this Joseph's brothers grew even more savagely jealous and hated what they thought was his pride. But his father did not forget the dream.

One day, as the brothers were minding their father's sheep on the plains, Jacob sent Joseph out to look for them and to tell him whether everything was all right. Joseph set out in search of them, and a man he met told him where their flocks were grazing.

The brothers saw Joseph a long way off and recognized him by his robe. "Here comes the dreamer," they said. "Now is our chance to kill him, for we are alone and no one will ever know. We can throw his body into this deep pit and say that a wild beast has eaten him."

But Reuben, the eldest of the brothers, felt sorry for Joseph, and persuaded the others to spare his life. They agreed instead to beat him and throw him into the pit, hoping he would die of exposure. But Reuben intended to come back on his own to rescue Joseph.

So when Joseph came up to his brothers expecting to be welcomed, they turned on him instead and beat him cruelly. Then they stripped off his robe and threw him into the nearby pit.

Then they sat down to eat, and while they were resting they saw a caravan in the distance, carrying spices southwards to Egypt. Then Judah said, "I have an idea. Why don't we sell our brother to these merchants, instead of leaving him to die in this pit?"

So Joseph was pulled up out of the pit and sold to the merchants for twenty pieces of

silver. They took Joseph with them to Egypt, and sold him there as a slave.

When Reuben came back to the pit to rescue Joseph he found it empty. "The boy is lost," he cried out in distress. "Now how can I take him back to our father?" And he tore his clothes in sorrow.

Meanwhile, the others had killed a goat, and then taken Joseph's robe and dipped it in the goat's blood. They slashed the robe to bits, as if a wild beast had savaged it, and brought it to their father. "Look what we have found!" they cried. "Do you recognize it? Isn't this Joseph's robe?"

"Yes," Jacob replied sadly, "it *is* Joseph's robe. A wild beast has attacked him and torn him to pieces." And he wept and tore his clothes in sorrow for the son he had loved so well. His other children tried to comfort him, but it was useless. "I will go on mourning Joseph's death until the day I die," he said.

Joseph in Potiphar's House

THE merchants who had brought Joseph to Egypt offered him for sale in the slave market. He was called a *Hebrew*, which means "an immigrant from the other side of the river." Joseph was bought by Potiphar, the captain of Pharaoh's guard, and taken into his household as a slave.

But God took care of Joseph and guided him in all his work, so that he did very well and earned praise from his Egyptian master. Soon Potiphar made Joseph his personal servant; then he put him in charge of his whole household; finally, he left everything he had in Joseph's care. Potiphar began to work less and less and to leave more and more to his Hebrew slave.

Potiphar's wife had noticed that Joseph was young and handsome. She grew more and more attracted to him. Finally, one day, she asked him to sleep with her. Joseph refused at once. "Think of my master," he said. "He has entrusted everything he has to me. I cannot betray him or take anything from him."

This noble behaviour made Potiphar's wife love and admire him all the more, and she kept begging him to make love to her. But Joseph turned his back, and would have nothing to do with her. Then she grew very angry and decided to have her revenge on him. She told her husband that Joseph had come into her room and tried to make love to her. As proof of this she showed Potiphar Joseph's cloak, pretending that he had left

it behind in the struggle when she had fought to free herself from his embraces.

Potiphar believed his wife's lies, and was furious. He had Joseph thrown into prison at once. He was sent to the Round Tower where Pharaoh's own prisoners were held. But here too God took care of Joseph, so that he soon won the confidence of the governor and was put in charge of the other prisoners in the tower.

It so happened that Pharaoh's chief butler and his chief baker had angered their master and were sent to prison. They were put into the same Round Tower where Joseph was held, and the prison governor ordered Joseph to take care of them. He became their personal servant and was trusted by each of them, just as he had been by Potiphar.

One night, when they had been in prison some time, the chief butler and the chief baker each had a dream which made them extremely frightened. They wanted to find someone who could interpret their dreams for them. When Joseph saw how afraid they were, he said to them, "Tell me your dreams, and my God will help me interpret them."

The chief butler told his dream first:

"In my dream I saw a vine in front of me. It had three branches, covered in buds; then blossom appeared on the branches, and then the blossom ripened into grapes. Then I gathered the grapes and crushed them

directly into Pharaoh's glass·and gave the glass to him."

Joseph said to him, "The three branches mean three days. Within three days Pharaoh will call for you and restore you to your post, and you will serve him each night just as you used to do. But remember me when you are free again, and tell Pharaoh about me, so that I can get out of this tower. I have done nothing at all to deserve imprisonment."

Then it was the chief baker's turn to tell Joseph his dream, and he was filled with hope at the butler's good news.

"I too had a dream," he said, "and in it there were three baskets of white bread on my head. In the top basket there was every kind of food I have ever prepared for Pharaoh, and the birds were eating out of it as it rested on my head."

Joseph said, "Those three baskets also mean three days. Within three days Pharaoh will call for you, and then he will have you hanged from a tree until you are dead, and then the birds will come and peck away your flesh."

The baker waited in terror. The first day passed, and the second day too. On the third day, however, it was Pharaoh's birthday, a day on which he gave a feast for all his servants, and he ordered that the chief butler and the chief baker should be brought out of prison.

When they had been led before him, he said: "I shall restore my chief butler to his post, to serve me as he used to do. My chief baker, however, has done wrong and must die."

The baker was sentenced to be hanged, just as Joseph had foretold, and the birds came and ate the flesh from his bones.

The chief butler was delighted to be free and serving his master again, but he forgot all about Joseph in the prison, and did not speak about him to Pharaoh.

Pharaoh's Dreams

Two years went by, and still Joseph remained locked away in the Round Tower, waiting to be freed. It seemed he had been forgotten, not only by the chief butler, but by everyone.

Then one night Pharaoh had a dream: he was standing by the river Nile, when suddenly seven sleek, fat cows came up out of the river and started grazing on the land. Next Pharaoh saw seven more cows, looking very thin and scraggy, come up out of the river and stand among the seven fat cows. Then the thin cows started to fight the fat ones and ate them all up. The dream faded

away and Pharaoh awoke, deeply troubled.

Then he had a second dream: seven full and ripe ears of wheat were growing on one stalk, and immediately behind them were seven more ears of wheat, empty and shrivelled up by the wind. The empty ears seemed to swallow up the full ones, and again Pharaoh awoke and was afraid.

When morning came, he called together all the magicians and wise men of Egypt. He told them about his dreams, but not one of them could tell him what they meant. Then Pharaoh's chief butler suddenly remembered about Joseph, and he told Pharaoh how

Joseph had interpreted their dreams when he and the chief baker had been in prison, and how he had quite correctly predicted life for one of them and death for the other.

Pharaoh was impressed by this and sent for Joseph at once. He was brought out of the Round Tower and taken to court. When he had listened to Pharaoh's dream, he said:

"These two dreams are really one dream. God has told Pharaoh what he intends to do. The seven fat cows represent seven years, and the seven full ears of wheat mean the same seven years—these will be years of plenty. The seven thin cows also mean seven years, and the empty ears of wheat are those same seven years—and these years will be years of famine. This means that there will be seven years of good harvests and of great wealth, and then there will be seven years of drought and famine when nothing will grow and your animals will starve, and the whole land of Egypt will lie in ruins.

"Because God's will is set on this, it would be as well for you to lay in stores against these years of famine by appointing overseers and marshals in every part of the land to gather and store one fifth of every crop to feed you in the poor years. You must build new granaries and storehouses and they must be well guarded. This is the only way you will have enough food for the people during these years of famine. Only in this way can you save Egypt."

Pharaoh was amazed at the way Joseph interpreted his dreams, and also at the wise advice he gave. He said to Joseph:

"Since it is God who has made these things known to you, you are obviously possessed of unusually great wisdom and powers beyond those of other men. I appoint you to be in charge of my household, and all my people will do as you command. I hereby give you authority and power over the whole of Egypt."

Pharaoh took off his royal signet ring and put it on Joseph's finger to show that he was to be his viceroy. Then he sent for fine clothes for Joseph to wear and hung a golden chain of office around his neck. He gave him his viceroy's chariot to travel about in, and men would cry, "Make way!" when they saw him coming. Pharaoh also gave Joseph an Egyptian woman to be his wife, and a new Egyptian name.

Then God sent the Egyptian people seven years of rich and fruitful harvests, and Joseph had the grain gathered and stored in the cities. Great granaries were specially built to house it, until the grain was piled far and wide like the sand on the seashore—beyond all counting.

When the seven years of plenty had ended they were followed, as Joseph had foretold, by seven years of famine. There was famine in every country of the world, but Egypt alone was prepared for it and had enough grain in store to feed its people. And before the famine had ended people from all over the world had come to Joseph in Egypt, to buy wheat from him.

Joseph's Brothers in Egypt

WHEN Jacob heard that there was wheat to be bought in Egypt while the rest of the world was starving, he said to his sons, "Go to Egypt and buy some of this wheat and bring it back here so that we can all eat bread again."

Then Jacob's sons saddled their mules and set out for Egypt. They left their youngest brother, Benjamin, behind, for he was their father's favourite now that Joseph had gone, and Jacob was afraid that some harm might befall him on the way.

When Jacob's sons arrived in Egypt they presented themselves to Joseph, as the

governor of the land, and bowed low before him and asked for wheat. Joseph recognized his brothers at once, but he pretended not to know them, and spoke harshly to them. "Where are you from?" he asked. "From Canaan," they replied. "We have come to buy food."

They did not recognize Joseph at all, for they did not expect to see their brother ever again, and certainly not as Pharaoh's right-hand man, the most important man in Egypt.

"You are spies," Joseph said to them. "You have come to spy out Egypt's defences, and you must be punished."

"No, no, sir," his brothers protested, "we are not spies, we have just come to buy food. We are honest men, sir, twelve brothers from Canaan. The youngest has remained at home with our father, and the other has disappeared."

Now Joseph specially longed to see Benjamin again, for he was the youngest, and Rachel's only other son besides Joseph himself.

So he said to his brothers, "I will find out if you are telling the truth. Leave one of your brothers behind with me, take the food you need for your people, and go. If you bring your youngest brother back with you I shall know you are not spies, but honest men. Then I will let your other brother go, and you can all return home freely."

Then he took his brother Simeon as the hostage, and filled their sacks up with wheat, and they all went back to their father Jacob in Canaan.

Jacob did not want to lose Benjamin and he forbade the others to take him to Egypt. But soon the famine grew so bad that there was no food at all left in Canaan, and they were once again forced to go to Egypt to buy some. This time they took Benjamin with them, and Jacob sent gifts of balsam

and honey, myrrh and almonds, to the governor of Egypt, hoping to soften his heart towards his sons.

When Joseph saw that his brothers had brought Benjamin he was overjoyed and ordered a great feast to be prepared. "Is your father still alive?" he asked them. "Is he well?" "Yes, sir," they answered, "he is alive and well."

Then Joseph was overcome with tears, and he went and hid himself so they would not see him crying. But it was not the proper time for him to reveal himself as their brother, so he swallowed his tears and came back to them, and ordered the feast to be served.

When it was over Joseph had his brothers' sacks filled with wheat, and in Benjamin's sack he hid his own silver goblet underneath the grain.

At daybreak the next day the brothers left to start their journey, but before they had gone more than a few miles Joseph sent his steward after them, to accuse them of stealing his goblet. The steward searched their sacks, and of course the goblet was found in Benjamin's. The brothers insisted they knew nothing about it, and begged the steward to let their youngest brother go free.

"You'll have to ask my master about that," said the steward. So they all returned to the city to beg the Egyptian governor for mercy for Benjamin.

But Joseph said, "Because my goblet was found on him he must become my slave, but the rest of you may go free."

Then Judah came up to him and said, "Please listen, sir. You are as powerful as Pharaoh, so we beg you to understand our distress. If we leave our brother Benjamin here, our father, who is very old, will surely die of sorrow, for he will have lost the two sons he loved best. I beg you, let me take the boy's place here, and let him go free."

Joseph could contain himself no longer. He sent all his attendants away and said to them, "I am your brother Joseph, the brother you sold to the merchants. With God's help I have become great; I have saved men's lives and now I have saved yours too, for the sake of your descendants. Go back to our father in Canaan and tell him that the famine will go on for another five years. Bring him back with you to Egypt, and bring your flocks and your herds and everything you own. And hurry!"

Then he threw his arms around Benjamin and hugged him, and kissed each of his brothers, in turn and wept for joy.

Jacob Goes to Egypt

PHARAOH was glad when he heard that the brothers of Joseph, his trusted governor, had come to Egypt to buy wheat. He said to Joseph, "Tell your brothers to go back to Canaan with all the food they have bought here; say to them that they must tell your father that Joseph, the son he believed dead, is alive and has become mighty, second only after me.

"Bring your father to me," Pharaoh went on, "and I will give him and all your brothers the best land that there is to be had in Egypt, so that they can settle here and make this country their new home.

"Have my wagons prepared for them, to carry your brothers and their wives and children. Tell them not to regret leaving their homes and belongings behind in Canaan, for they will have ten times more once they are in Egypt."

So Joseph gave his brothers the wagons and food and new clothes they needed for the journey, and to Benjamin he gave extra robes and 300 pieces of silver. He also sent his father ten mules laden with riches from Egypt, and ten more to carry grain, bread and other food for the journey. Then he sent his brothers back to Canaan, telling them not to quarrel with each other on the way home.

When they reached their father's house, they called to him: "Joseph is still alive! He is governor over all the land of Egypt!"

Jacob almost fainted, for he could hardly believe their words. But then they told him the whole story, and when their father saw the wagons and the mules and the gifts that Joseph had sent him, he was full of joy.

"It's enough," he said to them. "Now I know that Joseph my son must still be alive after all, and I will go to Egypt and see him once more before I die."

So Jacob set out with all his household and everything that he had. On his way south he stopped at Beersheba to offer sacrifices of thanksgiving to God. And God spoke to him and said:

"Don't be afraid to go to Egypt, Jacob, for I will bring you back safely to your own land. Do you remember how, after you fought the angel on your way into Canaan, I changed your name to Israel? I did this because you are going to be the father of a great nation, and your twelve sons will be the founders of the twelve tribes of Israel."

When he heard they were coming, Joseph ordered his chariot to be made ready, and he went to meet his father at a place called Goshen. When at last they stood face to face after so many years, Joseph threw his arms around his father and wept, and Jacob wept too and held him close to him. Then he said to Joseph, "Now that I have seen your face again, I am ready to die whenever God pleases."

Joseph told Pharaoh that his father and his brothers had arrived in Egypt, and Pharaoh called them to him and said, "This land is yours to live in wherever you like. Go and find the greenest and most fertile places along the Nile and settle in them."

Pharaoh knew that these Hebrews would bring valuable skills and experience to his country, and that they would work hard to make Egypt a richer place.

Jacob was proud of his sons. He raised his hands over Pharaoh, and blessed him.

The Famine

THE famine raged in every country; both Egypt and Canaan suffered terribly. Joseph, as governor of the land, collected all the silver in Egypt and in Canaan in exchange for the wheat which the people bought, and stored it in Pharaoh's treasury. When all the silver in Egypt and in Canaan had been collected and taken away, the Egyptians said to Joseph, "Give us bread or we shall die. We have no more silver to buy wheat."

Joseph said, "If your silver is all gone, you can bring me your herds and I will give you bread in exchange." So the people brought their herds to Joseph and he gave them bread. For a whole year the people were able to feed off the bread they had exchanged for their livestock. But still the famine went on raging, and finally the people came back to Joseph and said:

"My lord, our silver and our cattle now all belong to Pharaoh, and we have nothing left but our bodies and our land. Take us and the land we live on in payment for bread, and we will serve Pharaoh in bondage. For if we have no food we shall die, and if we die there will be no one to farm our land

and it will become desert once again."

So Joseph bought up all the land in Egypt for Pharaoh, and he set the people working as slaves from one end of the land to the other. He gave them seed so that they could plant new crops, and he made them give one fifth of every crop to Pharaoh.

At last the time came when Joseph's father Jacob was nearing his death. His sons all gathered round his bed to receive his last blessing. Joseph had brought his two sons, Manasseh and Ephraim, who had been born to him in Egypt. "These are my sons, the gift of God," he said to his father. Then Jacob held the boys close to him and kissed them and said, "I had not expected ever to see my son's face again, and now God has allowed me to see his sons as well." And he blessed them in turn. Then he blessed each one of his own twelve sons and foretold that they would be the founders of the twelve tribes of Israel.

"When I am dead," he said to them, "don't leave my body in Egypt. Bury me in Canaan with my forefathers." And with these words he died.

Pharaoh ordered a period of mourning for Jacob all over Egypt, lasting for 70 days. All the leaders of Egypt followed Joseph and his brothers as they went to bury Jacob in Canaan, in the land which God had given to him and his descendants for ever.

The Birth of Moses

PHARAOH invited Jacob's twelve sons to come and live in Egypt. They worked hard as the years went by, and their families grew large enough to be known as tribes and settled all over Egypt. They were known as Israelites, from the name God had given Jacob long before.

But they were not happy people. They still lived in Goshen, the fertile district that had been given to them by the friendly Pharaoh who had invited their forefathers to come to Egypt. But now the Egyptians made them work hard, clearing the land and digging channels through the fields so that the crops could get water from the Nile. They were made to bake bricks, too, for a great new city was being built.

A new Pharaoh had come to the throne, who remembered nothing about Joseph. "These Israelites outnumber us," he told the Egyptians, "and they are more powerful than we are. We must protect ourselves against them, for if a war breaks out they will join our enemies, and take over our country."

So Pharaoh made slaves of the Israelites, and tried to break their spirit with hard work. But it seemed that the worse they were treated the more children they had. Their tribes grew larger and larger, and the Egyptians feared and hated them even more.

Then Pharaoh sent for the Hebrew midwives and said, "When you are helping the Hebrew women give birth, watch if the child is a boy or a girl. If it is a girl, let her live, but if it is a boy, kill him instantly."

The midwives knew Pharaoh was asking them to do wrong, so they let the boys live. Then Pharaoh ordered his own people to drown every newborn Hebrew boy in the Nile.

One woman, though, a descendant of Jacob's son Levi, gave birth to a fine boy, and managed to hide him from the Egyptians. When the baby was three months old the Levite woman could not hide him any longer. She bought a basket woven of rushes and made it watertight with clay and tar. Then she laid the baby in it and hid the basket in the reeds of the river bank. She went home in tears, but her daughter waited nearby to see what would happen.

Presently Pharaoh's daughter came down to bathe in the Nile. She noticed the basket hidden in the reeds and sent a servant to fetch it. When she opened it, the baby was crying and at once she felt sorry for it. "Why," she said, "it is a Hebrew baby someone has left to die."

At that moment the boy's sister ran up. "Shall I fetch a Hebrew woman who can nurse the baby for you?" she asked. Pharaoh's daughter wanted to keep the child, so she sent the girl to find a nurse. The girl ran and fetched the baby's own mother.

"Here is a child I have found," the princess said to her. "I want you to nurse him and take care of him for me." The woman did not tell the princess who she was—she was too happy at having saved her baby's life. So she took her child and looked after him until he was old enough to serve Pharaoh's daughter. When the Egyptian princess saw the boy she was so pleased with him that she adopted him as her own son. She called him Moses because the name meant that he was someone who had been drawn out of the water.

Moses in Midian

Time passed, and Moses grew up in the household of Pharaoh's daughter. He was always treated with respect because the princess had adopted him, but as he grew older he realized that he was not an Egyptian by birth but an Israelite, and that the rest of his people were living in misery as the Egyptians' slaves.

One day he went out to watch his fellow Hebrews at work making bricks and doing the heavy work in the fields, and he saw an Egyptian strike a slave to the ground. Anger rose in him, and he struck the Egyptian so hard that he killed him.

Then, fearful of Pharaoh's anger, he hid the body of the Egyptian by burying it in the sand.

Next day Moses saw two Hebrew slaves fighting each other. "Why are you fighting your fellow countryman?" he asked the one who had begun it. "Who made you our judge?" retorted the slave. "Do you mean to murder me as you murdered that Egyptian?" Then Moses grew afraid that everybody knew what he had done, and he decided to flee the country.

When Pharaoh heard that Moses had killed one of his guards he ordered that he be arrested and executed. But fortunately Moses had already managed to escape into the land of Midian, which lay far to the east of Egypt, beyond the Red Sea. He knew nobody there, but he was safe from Pharaoh's anger.

One day he came to a small village, and

sat down by its well to rest. The land was poor, and there was hardly any grass because it was so dry. Moses saw seven girls who were driving their sheep up to be watered, and the other shepherds at the well told him they were the daughters of Jethro, the village priest. The water in the well was very low, and the other shepherds, who were all men, told the girls to wait until they had given their own flocks all the water they needed.

"That's not fair," thought Moses, who had been watching, and he hurried forward to defend the girls. Pushing the shepherds

roughly aside, he himself filled up the water troughs so that the girls' sheep could drink, and the shepherds even began to help him do this, because they were afraid of his strength.

When the daughters of Jethro came home, their father said, "What brings you back so early today? Didn't you go to the pasture where the water in the well is low and the men fight you for it?"

"Yes," said Zipporah, one of his daughters. "We went there, and the men were rough. But a stranger dressed like an Egyptian came and took our part. He fought the men off, then he drew the water for us himself, and gave it to our sheep."

"Where is this man?" said the priest. "You shouldn't have left him behind. Go and invite him here to eat and drink with us, and rest in our house."

That was how Moses came to live in Jethro's house. Later Jethro gave him Zipporah as his wife, and she bore Moses two sons. He settled down in Midian and looked after his father-in-law's flocks.

But he could never forget Egypt and his fellow countrymen who were still held in captivity there as slaves.

The Voice from the Burning Bush

THE years went by and there was a new Pharaoh in Egypt, but the Israelites were no better off. At last their prayers and cries of suffering reached God and reminded him of the promise he had made to Abraham so long before.

Moses was still living in Midian, minding his father-in-law's flocks. One day, as he was leading his sheep to graze in wild pastures, he came to Horeb, the mountain sacred to God, and he saw an extraordinary thing. A bush on the mountainside was burning, but although the flames came from it, the bush itself was not burned.

As Moses stood there marvelling, the voice of God called to him out of the fire, "Moses, Moses," and he replied, "Here I am."

"Don't come any closer," God said to him, "and take your shoes off, for you are standing on holy ground. I am the God of Abraham, the God of Isaac, and the God of Jacob." And Moses did as God told him, but he covered up his face, for he was afraid to look directly at God.

Then God said, "I have seen the sufferings of my people in Egypt; I have heard them crying out to me, and now I have come to rescue them from the Egyptians and bring them to the good and fruitful land where the Canaanites and the Hittites live. Come–I will send you to Pharaoh, and you shall bring the children of Israel safely out of Egypt."

Moses was afraid. He said to God, "Who am I, to be given so much responsibility?"

"Don't be afraid," God said to him, "I will help you, and to prove that I have sent you, when you have brought your people safely out of Egypt, you will all come here to this mountain to worship me."

Then Moses said, "If I go and tell the Israelites that the God of their forefathers has sent me, they will ask me his name, and then what shall I say?"

God answered, "Tell them that God has sent you, their God Jehovah, the God of their fathers Abraham and Isaac and Jacob, for this is my name for ever."

But Moses still said, "I don't think they will believe me."

"What is that in your hand?" God asked him.

"A staff of wood," he replied.

God said, "Throw it on the ground," and Moses did so, and at once it became a wriggling snake. He jumped back in horror, but God said, "Pick it up by the tail." Trembling, Moses did, and it turned back into a staff again.

Then God said, "Put your hand inside your cloak," and Moses did. When he drew his hand out again, it was all white and covered with sores. Then God told him to do it again, and when he pulled his hand out, God had healed it completely.

God said to Moses, "I am giving you these signs to prove to the people that you are my messenger and that I, and I alone, have sent you to help and guide them."

Pharaoh and the Israelites

God said to Moses, "Now go back to Egypt and bring the Israelites out of slavery to freedom."

But Moses replied, "O Lord, I am not the man you are looking for. I have never been able to speak well. I hesitate in my speech, and cannot find the right words to rouse people." God said, "Who do you think makes a man able to speak well? Who makes him dumb or deaf, or clear-sighted or blind? It is I, the Lord. I will help you when you speak and tell you what to say."

But Moses still protested and said, "No, Lord, please send someone else." Then God said, "You have a brother named Aaron. He will do the speaking for you. He is on his way to meet you now. I will help you both and tell you what to do. He will speak to the people for you and you will tell him what to say."

So Moses went home and said goodbye to his wife and sons. Then, holding the staff of God in his hand, he set out for Egypt. Aaron his brother came and met him on the way, and when Moses had told him everything that had happened, the two of them went to the leaders of the Israelites and called all the people together. Aaron told them what God had said to his brother, and Moses showed them the signs. And everyone believed that God had heard them and would free them from slavery, and they

all kneeled down and gave thanks to God.

Then Moses and Aaron went to Pharaoh and said:

"The Lord God of Israel has said, 'Let my people go so that they can offer sacrifices to me.' Let our people go, O Pharaoh."

But Pharaoh replied, "Moses and Aaron, how dare you call my slaves away from their work? Your people already outnumber the Egyptians in this land, yet you want them to stop working!"

That same day Pharaoh gave orders that the Israelites should be made to work even

[60]

harder. "Don't supply any more straw for them to bake bricks with," he told his overseers. "Make them find their own. But remember—I want the same number of bricks made as before."

So the Israelites were made to search the land to find stubble for their bricks. But of course they could not produce as many as before, and their overseers beat them. The Israelite leaders went to Pharaoh and asked him why he treated them so harshly.

"You are a lazy bunch," Pharaoh replied. "You talk about going to offer sacrifices to your God, but it's just an excuse for you not to work."

Then the Israelites blamed Moses and Aaron for causing them so much misery. Once more the two brothers went to Pharaoh to ask for the Israelites' freedom. Aaron threw down his staff at Pharaoh's feet, and it turned into a snake. At this, Pharaoh summoned his own wise men and magicians and they threw down their staffs, and these too became snakes. Then Aaron's snake gobbled up each of the others in turn—but still Pharaoh would not set the Israelites free.

[61]

The Plagues of Egypt

GOD said to Moses, "Pharaoh has refused to let my people go. Go and strike the river Nile with your staff, and the water in all Egypt's rivers and wells will be changed into blood. The fish will die and the rivers will stink, and the Egyptians won't be able to drink the water. There will be blood all through the land of Egypt–I will show Pharaoh that I am God."

Moses did as God commanded, but still Pharaoh would not set the Israelites free.

Then God said to Moses, "Go again to Pharaoh and say, 'Let my people go. If you refuse, I will plague your land with frogs. They will come up from the rivers into your house, into your bed, into your ovens and into your bread. They will climb all over you and your people.'" And the frogs swarmed all over the land. But still Pharaoh would not set the people free.

God said to Moses, "Stretch out your staff and strike the dust on the ground, and the dust will fly up and change into mosquitoes. These will sting every animal and every Egyptian in the land." When Pharaoh saw the plague of mosquitoes, he said to his magicians, "Surely your magic is as good as the Hebrews'? Get rid of these mosquitoes!" But the magicians were frightened. "This is no ordinary magic," they said to

Pharaoh, "God has done this to the Egyptians." But still Pharaoh would not listen to them.

"Let my people go," Moses said to Pharaoh. "If you don't, God will send down swarms of flies. Your houses will be filled with them, but not the houses of *my* people." The air over Egypt was filled with flies–but still Pharaoh would not let the Israelites go.

Then God struck the herds of Egypt down with a sickness so bad that most of the beasts died. He sent a fine dust over the land, and the dust settled on men and animals alike and turned into boils and sores that festered on their bodies. But still Pharaoh would not listen.

Then God sent a great hailstorm with hail the size of rocks; the hail killed every man and beast that was out in the open fields– but still Pharaoh would not listen.

Then God said to Moses, "Stretch out your staff and locusts will come and eat up what few crops the hail has left," and Moses did so, and such swarms of locusts descended on Egypt that the whole land was black with them. They ate until there was nothing green left throughout the land.

Then God said to Moses, "Stretch out your staff towards the sky, and there will be darkness over the land." The darkness that came was so heavy that it could be felt, and for three days there was no light at all.

Then at last Pharaoh was prepared to let the Israelites go, but he said they must leave their herds behind. "No," Moses said to him, "God has spared our animals because we need them to support ourselves and to sacrifice to him. Our flocks and herds must go with us."

Then Pharaoh was furious. "Get out and never let me see you again," he said to Moses. "I will never let your people go."

The Institution of the Passover

GOD said to Moses, "I will send down one last plague on Egypt, and then Pharaoh will let you go. So I want you to begin a new year, starting from tonight, the last night that you will all be held in slavery. From now on this month will become the first month of your new year. I want you to call the people together and give them my instructions.

"On the tenth day of this month each man must choose a lamb or a kid for his family—one for each household, or if the household is too small for one animal, neighbours can join together and share. They must share the cost out equally, to take account of the number of people in each family and the amount that each one of them eats.

"The lamb or kid must be the best in the flock, but if need be you can take a sheep or a goat instead. You must keep it safe until the fourteenth day of this month, and then you must all meet together and slaughter your animals in the time between evening and nightfall.

"You must take some of the blood and smear it on each of the doorposts and on the

lintel of every house in which a lamb is eaten. The meat must be roasted over the fire, and you must eat unleavened, flat bread with it and green herbs. You must not eat any of it raw or boiled in water; the entire beast must be roasted, with its head and its guts too. Not a scrap of it must be left over until the next day, or it may become tainted, so if anything is left, you must burn it at once.

"I want you to eat this meal in a special way—with your belts fastened, your sandals on your feet, and your staffs in your hands—and you must eat it quickly in memory of the night when I told you to hurry away from Egypt and be free once again. This meal is to be called the Lord's Passover, for tonight I will kill every first-born thing in Egypt, but I will pass over all the homes of the Israelites in safety.

"Keep this day as a day of remembrance and a special festival. Keep it from generation to generation, wherever you live, for all time.

"For seven days you must eat unleavened bread that has no yeast in it to make it rise, for you must eat nothing that is fermented. Anyone who eats bread that has risen will be called an outlaw. On the first day of the seven you must all gather for a service, and on the seventh day you must have another service. On these days no work must be done, save what has to be done in order to provide food for everyone to eat.

"I want the Israelites to keep this feast for themselves and their children for ever. When they enter the promised land of Canaan, they must do exactly as I have said. Then when their children ask them the meaning of this ritual, they can tell them, 'It is the Passover, to honour God and celebrate the time he passed over the houses of the Israelites that night in Egypt when he killed the Egyptians but spared us, and freed us from our captivity.'"

[65]

The Night of the Passover

THEN God sent Moses to warn Pharaoh. "At midnight tonight," Moses told him, "the God of Israel will go out among the Egyptians, and every first-born creature in the land will die—the eldest son of Pharaoh himself and the eldest son of the slave at the mill and the first-born of every animal in the fields.

"The whole land of Egypt will cry out in dreadful anguish, a cry of sorrow more terrible than any that has ever been heard, or will ever be heard again. But not one man or beast belonging to the Israelites will be hurt – not even one dog's tongue will be so much as scratched."

But Pharaoh still would not set the people free.

Then God gave Moses instructions for the Israelites, and he called all the elders of his people together and gave them God's commands:

"Each man must take a sheep or a kid for his household and kill it and prepare it as a sacrifice to our God. Then take a bunch of marjoram, dip it into the blood and smear blood onto the lintel of each door and on the two doorposts. Nobody must use the door of his house until morning, for tonight God will go through the land of Egypt and kill every first-born son, but when he sees the mark on each door he will pass over it and will do no harm to anyone inside that house."

The people of Israel listened to Moses. They kneeled down and worshipped God, then they hurried away to do as God had commanded them.

By midnight that night God had struck down every first-born in Egypt, from

Pharaoh's own son in the palace to the first-born of the captive in his prison.

Before the night was over a terrible cry of anguish and mourning was heard all over Egypt, because death had come to every single family in the land.

While it was still dark Pharaoh sent for Moses and Aaron. "Get up and go," he cried. "Serve your God and let us alone. Take your sheep and your cattle and leave my land for ever—and as you go, remember

to ask your God to send me his blessing instead of this dreadful curse."

The Egyptians urged the Israelites to hurry because they wanted to get rid of them before anything worse happened. The Israelites hurried to leave in case Pharaoh might change his mind. They snatched up their belongings, and because their bread dough had not had time to rise, they wrapped up the basins with the dough in them inside their cloaks, just as they were. Then they left Egypt for ever.

The Crossing of the Red Sea

When Pharaoh heard that all the 600,000 Israelites had gone off with their families and their cattle, he regretted letting them go. He hardly had any slaves left to do the work. He ordered every war chariot in Egypt to be made ready and galloped after the Israelites, taking with him all the regiments of his cavalry and his infantry. It was a mighty army and the thunder of the horses' hooves and the rumble of the chariot wheels could be heard a long way off.

ONCE the Israelites had left Egypt they rested and made fires on which to bake their bread. They baked the dough just as it was, kneaded flat, because there was no time to let it rise. In later times men and women would be proud to eat this unleavened bread in memory of the Israelites fleeing through the desert to freedom.

Moses did not take the people back to Canaan by the shortest way, because that would have meant crossing through the land of the Philistines. The Israelites, weak after their long years of captivity, were no match for that fierce tribe. The Philistines would have killed them and driven off their flocks and herds in triumph.

"I will protect my chosen people from danger," said God, "and guide them safely through places where no man lives."

As they marched, a cloud of smoke went ahead of them showing the way, and at night it was a cloud of fire that reached up into the sky.

By these signs God guided the Israelites through the wilderness to the shore of the Red Sea. Here the cloud stood still, and they camped because God commanded it.

From their camp by the Red Sea the Israelites saw the great army of Egyptians appear in the distance.

"Help us, Lord!" they cried out in terror. Then they turned on Moses.

"Why did you take us out of Egypt to die like this?" they complained. "We would have been better off living as slaves."

Then God said to Moses, "Tell your people not to be afraid. They must pick up all their possessions and follow you. Raise your staff in front of you, and stretch it out over the sea, and I promise that the waters will part in two and you will be able to walk on dry land right across the sea bed. When you are all safely across, I will fill the Egyptians' hearts with hatred of you. They will rush after you, and then I shall destroy them."

Then the cloud of smoke that was God's signal moved from in front of the Israelites to behind them, so that it lay between them

were escaping from them, they rushed after them into the sea, with their horses and chariots, their infantry and cavalry. But their chariot wheels sank in the wet sand, and the horses and men were bogged down.

"God himself is fighting for Israel!" the Egyptians cried. They looked around them and what they saw filled them with terror. They were trapped between the two great walls of water.

Panic broke out. Soldiers threw down their weapons and tried to run for their lives. But their feet sank deeper and deeper into the sand. The horses reared in the chariot shafts, whinnying and pounding the air.

The commanders made one last effort. They ordered the men to return to their chariots and wrench the wheels free.

But it was no use. They could move neither forwards nor backwards; they were all stuck fast in the middle of the Red Sea.

Then God commanded Moses to stretch out his staff over the sea again, and the walls of water gave way. With a mighty roar the sea water swept over Pharaoh's army, over his chariots and over his horses, so that every man and beast was drowned.

When the Israelites saw such a great army destroyed, and all the bodies piled along the shore, they feared their God more than ever, and respected Moses his servant, too, for they knew that it was God who had saved the children of Israel from the power of Pharaoh.

Then Miriam, the sister of Moses and of Aaron, picked up her tambourine and began a dance of joy. And all the women followed her, dancing to the sound of their tambourines and singing:

"Sing to the Lord for he is triumphant;
The horse and his rider are thrown into the sea.
Sing to the Lord for he is my refuge;
My God and my strength he shall always be."

and the Egyptians, hiding them from the Egyptians so that they could not see what was happening.

Moses stretched out his staff towards the sea, and a strong wind started to blow. It blew all night, so hard that it pushed back the sea water and made the sea bed into dry land. The Israelites were able to walk across on the sea bed, with high walls of water on either side of them.

When the Egyptians saw the Israelites

The Israelites Find Food

THE people of Israel left the Red Sea and marched for three days into the wilderness, searching for water to drink. At last they came to a place where there were pools of standing water. Eagerly, the people threw themselves down to drink from the pools but the water was so bitter that they could not swallow it. "Give us water," they begged Moses. Then God showed Moses a log, and when he threw it into the water, it became fresh and good and the people drank it thankfully.

It was there that God gave the people a rule for life. "If you will obey me," he told them through Moses, "If you will listen to my commands and obey them, I will spare you the suffering I have heaped on the Egyptians; for I am a healer."

The Israelites travelled on, but soon they ran out of food, and there was none to be found.

The Israelites complained to Moses, "If only we had stayed in Egypt, where at least there was plenty to eat! Out here, we are going to starve to death."

God said to Moses, "I will rain down bread from heaven. Each day I want your people to go out and gather in all they need for that day. On the sixth day I shall send twice as much as on the other days so that

they can rest on the seventh day, and still obey my commands."

Then Moses and Aaron told the people, "You will soon be sure it was God who brought you out of Egypt. Trust him—he will give you meat to eat in the evening, and bread in the morning."

While they were speaking, the Israelites looked up and saw a great cloud of fire over the wilderness, which reassured them that God was present.

That evening a flock of quails flew over the camp and settled so thickly that they covered the ground. The people killed them and had meat to eat, as God had promised. In the morning the dew lay thickly all around the tents, and when it had lifted, there were flakes like hoarfrost all over the ground.

"What is this?" the wondering people asked Moses.

"That is the bread God has given you," Moses replied. "You must collect as much as you can, and everyone should have one measure for each person in his tent. But no one must keep any until tomorrow." They all did this, and although some gathered more than others, there was just the right amount for each person to eat his fill.

Some of the Israelites did try to keep it overnight, but it went bad and stank, and Moses was angry with them.

On the sixth day they gathered twice as much as on the other days, so that they could rest on the seventh day. Some people did go out to look for food on the seventh day, but they could not find any. Then God was angry. "I have given you enough food for today because I want you to stay home," he said to them. "This is my special day, a day of rest for everyone."

The Israelites called their new food *manna*. It was white, and it tasted like a wafer made with honey. They were to eat it all the way to the promised land.

[72]

The Water from the Rock

MOSES and Aaron went on leading the Israelites through the wilderness, back to the promised land, but at times there was bitterness between the people and their two leaders.

"There is nothing to drink in this wilderness," they cried. "Give us water to drink with our manna—we're dying of thirst."

"Trust God," Moses kept replying. "He will help you."

But the people grew angry. "Why did you bring us out of Egypt," they demanded, "just to let us all die here of thirst?"

Then Moses prayed to God, because he was afraid they would kill him.

"Go forward, Moses," God answered him. "Go on ahead of the others and take some of the leaders of the people with you—and don't forget your staff. You will find me waiting for you by the rock on Mount Horeb where I first spoke to you. Strike the rock with your staff, and water will pour out of it. I will bring the people after you to this rock so that they can drink and be satisfied."

Moses did exactly as God commanded. When he had reached Mount Horeb he gathered the Israelite leaders around him and struck the rock with his staff. Water came gushing up out of it, and every one of the Israelites came up in turn and drank as much as he wanted.

The Defeat of the Amalekites

THE people of Israel had walked a long way from Egypt, but they had even further still to go, and they were tired and thirsty. Slowly the gap between the strong and the weak grew wider; the oldest and the youngest fell behind, exhausted, and the sick came last of all.

Suddenly a fierce tribe of warriors, the Amalekites, attacked them from the rear. They killed the old and sick who were straggling behind. Then they challenged the other Israelites to a formal battle the following day.

That evening Moses called a young man named Joshua, the son of Nun, to his tent. Young as he was, Joshua was a brave and skilful fighter. Moses said to him:

"I want you to pick the best men from among our people, and lead them in battle tomorrow. While you fight the Amalekites on these plains, I will take my stand on top of the hill with the staff of God in my hand. I will see everything you do, and God will guide you."

The next morning Joshua called the men he had picked, and, taking their weapons, they marched onto the plains. Joshua gave them his instructions for the battle that was about to take place, and they waited for the Amalekite army to appear.

Meanwhile, Moses had called Aaron and another man he trusted, named Hur, to come with him. Together they climbed to the top of the hill from which they could see both the Israelite army and the clouds of

dust in the distance which meant that the Amalekites were approaching.

Joshua gave the signal to attack and, shouting their battle cries, the Israelites threw themselves at the Amalekites, who fought back fiercely. The battle raged, and for a time it looked as if neither side was gaining any ground.

Then Moses held up his staff as a sign to his people that they would conquer through God's help. A great strength seemed to flow through the Israelites and they broke right through the Amalekite lines. But after a time Moses' arm grew tired, and he lowered his staff again. Then the Amalekites pressed

forward and regained their lost ground.

It seemed that whenever Moses raised his staff the Amalekites would fall back and flee before the Israelites, crying out in fear, only to return, fighting even more fiercely, as soon as the Israelite forces slackened. For the staff was heavy, and Moses' arms kept getting tired. He would have to lower his staff—and then the power of God left his men, and the Amalekites had the advantage again.

Realizing what was happening, Aaron and Hur put a stone under Moses so that he could sit down; then they stood on either side of him and held up his hands for him. With this added support, Moses' arms never wavered again, and by sunset Joshua and the Israelites had beaten the Amalekites and driven them far into the wilderness.

The long battle was over. But before he rested, Moses built an altar to God, promising to keep the memory of the victory over the evil Amalekites for all time to come.

Jethro Advises Moses

ONE day, when Moses and the Israelites had pitched their tents near Mount Horeb, a man called to Moses: "Jethro, your father-in-law, is riding into camp with your wife and your two sons!"

Moses greeted the old priest and embraced his wife and sons. Then he led them into his tent, and they talked of all that had happened since he had left Midian. Jethro said:

"God has indeed done wonderful things, for he has set the people of Israel free from their slavery in Egypt. Now I know that he is the greatest of all gods."

Next day Jethro watched Moses at work among his people. Men and women crowded around him from morning till night, asking him questions and expecting him to settle their arguments. God guided Moses in his replies, and gave him laws for the people to follow at all times.

Jethro said to his son-in-law: "I can see that you speak to God for the people and teach them his laws. But the job is exhausting you—it is more than any one man can do. You must choose some other capable men to help you. Each of them can be responsible for a particular group of the people and they can act as judges and settle the simpler cases. Only the more difficult ones need then be brought to you, and this would keep you free for the work that you alone can do."

Moses took the advice and it worked well.

[76]

The Ten Commandments

IT was now nearly three months since the Israelites had left Egypt. They had been travelling through the wilderness of Sinai, and by the time they reached the foot of Mount Sinai they were tired.

Moses told them to pitch their tents in the plain beneath the mountain, and while they made their camp and gathered brushwood to build fires, he himself climbed up the slopes to the mountaintop. There the voice of God spoke to him and said:

"At this place, on this mountain, I will begin to make the Israelites into my chosen people. I have brought them safely out of Egypt where they were Pharaoh's slaves. Now I will give them, through you, laws and commandments that will rule them every day of their lives. They must obey me from the day they are born until the day they die. If they do all that I tell them to do, I will make them into a holy nation, for they are the people I have chosen to be my special possession. Go now, and tell this to your people."

Moses came back down the mountain to the plains below. He called the elders, who were the leaders of the people, together, and told them what God had said.

"Whatever God has said, we will do," the people cried out, and Moses climbed back up the mountain, and again found himself in the presence of God.

"Go, then," God told Moses when he had heard what the people said, "go back to the people and tell them to prepare themselves for what is to come. Tell them to purify themselves, to wash themselves and their clothes, and to clear their thoughts for two days. On the third day I will come down onto Mount Sinai and speak to them. But not one of them must go near the mountain in the meantime."

The people did as Moses told them, waiting eagerly for the days to pass. They built a barrier around the mountain, to show that its slopes were holy ground.

On the morning of the third day there was a storm with thunder and lightning, and a dark cloud covered Mount Sinai. Suddenly a trumpet sounded, so loudly that it seemed to fill the air, and the people in the camp beneath the mountain trembled with fear.

Moses led the people out to the foot of Mount Sinai, and the sound of the trumpet grew louder and louder around them. Then God came down like a fire onto Sinai, and the whole top of the mountain was wrapped in dense clouds of smoke as if it were a volcano erupting.

Then Moses spoke to God. The Israelites standing around him heard God's answers as a peal of thunder so loud that it hurt their ears, and they threw themselves to the earth in terror.

But Moses heard God calling him to climb the mountain yet again and talk to him. The watching Israelites saw their leader climb upwards, higher and higher, until he disappeared into the smoke that covered the mountaintop, and they trembled.

These are the rules God gave Moses for the Israelites to follow. They are known as the Ten Commandments.

"I am the Lord your God: you must have no other god, but me.

"You must not worship anything you have made yourselves, nor must you worship statues or pictures or images of anything that is in the sky or in the earth or beneath the earth. I am your God and I say that you must worship the being that is me, and only me. If you break this commandment I shall punish not just you but your children and your children's children. But I shall always be kind and merciful to the people who love me and obey my commandments.

"You must not call on the name of God without good reason, nor use it wrongly or without respect.

"Remember to keep the seventh day holy. On six days you can work and do all that you have to do, but the seventh day is my Sabbath. On this day you must not work, nor must any member of your family, or your household, or your animals, or even the stranger staying in your house. For in six days I made the heavens and the earth and the sea and all that is in them, and on the seventh day I rested. So I blessed the seventh day and made it a day of rest for ever.

"Respect and honour your father and your mother.

"You must not murder another human being.

"You must not sleep with another man's wife.

"You must not steal.

"You must not tell lies nor must you give evidence that is false.

"You must not long for anyone else's possessions and wish that you owned them yourself—do not envy another man's house, nor his wife, nor his servant, nor his cow, nor his donkey, nor anything else he has.

Remember, it is his, not yours."

Then God gave Moses more laws to guide the people in their daily lives. He said:

"You must love the Lord your God with all your heart and with all your soul and with all your strength. Teach your children to love me as you do, and I will reward you.

"And if any kind of hurt is done to you, you must pay back a life for a life, an eye for an eye, a tooth for a tooth, a hand for a hand, a burn for a burn, and a wound for a wound.

"Do not let yourself be led into doing something you know to be wrong because the majority of people favour it.

"Do not be unkind to anyone who is a stranger among you. Remember how you yourselves felt when you were strangers in Egypt.

"Sow your land and harvest the crops for six years running, but the seventh year let the land lie fallow and rest, so that it will be richer when you come to sow it again.

"Every first-born thing belongs to me. This applies to the males of all your herds and flocks, and to your first-born sons too. You must offer each first-born to me, and then buy it back again. Be sure never to come into my presence without an offering in your hands."

At last the watching people saw Moses coming back down the mountainside. They gathered around him to hear what God had said. But Moses spent a long time in his tent writing down all the commandments God had given him. Then he built an altar at the foot of Mount Sinai, and ordered bulls to be killed as sacrifices to God. Some of their blood he poured into basins and set on the altar; some he poured on the stones of the altar itself. Then Moses read God's commandments so that everyone could hear.

"We will do exactly as God has ordered us," the people shouted joyfully.

The Ark of the Covenant

"SEND your people back to their camp, and Aaron and Hur can look after their needs while you stay with me," God said to Moses, and he commanded him to climb the mountain once more.

So Moses went up again into the fire which burned at the top of the mountain and hung like a cloud around it. He stayed in God's presence for 40 days and 40 nights, and God spoke to him all the time.

"Tell the Israelites," God said, "to collect a special offering to be given to me. Take it from everyone who is willing to give it. Take gold and silver, and bronze and yarn and fine linen. Take leather, oil and spices, and jewels and powder to make incense with.

"I want them to build me a shrine so that I can always be present among you, my chosen people.

"I want them to build me an ark, a chest of acacia wood four feet long and two and a half feet broad and high. Overlay it with gold, outside and inside, and put a band of gold all round it. Cast four rings of gold for it and fasten them to its four supports, two rings on one side and two rings on the other. Then carve poles of acacia wood and overlay them with gold, and slip the poles through the rings at the side of the ark so that it can be carried. The poles must always rest in the rings; they must never be taken out.

"Inside the ark you must keep the laws that I have given you.

"Make a cover for it out of pure gold, four

feet long and two and a half feet wide. Make two winged creatures out of gold for the two ends of the cover, one at one end and one at the other. The wings of these creatures must be outstretched and spread over the cover, and they must be facing one another over the top of the cover.

"Inside the ark you must place the laws that I give you. In that place you must put the two stone tablets with my laws written

on them which I will give you, and there I will always be present to meet you and tell you what the Israelites must do.

"Make a table out of acacia wood overlaid with gold, and make poles so that the table too can be carried. Make bowls, pitchers and cups out of gold to stand on the table and to hold your offerings to me. Always keep an offering of bread on the table—it will be a sign that I am present among you.

"Make a lampstand out of gold with seven branches and a lamp hanging from each one.

"Make a tabernacle out of wood, draped with hangings of linen and skins, and hang a curtain of purple and red linen inside it. Put the ark inside the tabernacle, with the curtain hanging in front to screen it like a treasure—for the space behind the curtain will be called the Holy of Holies."

The Making of the Golden Calf

W HEN Moses was so long coming down from the mountain the Israelites thought something had happened to him. Their leaders gathered around his brother Aaron and said:

"This man Moses who brought us out of Egypt seems to have disappeared and we don't know what has become of him. We need a new god to lead us."

Aaron told them to take the gold ornaments that their women wore and bring them to him. The people stripped themselves of their earrings and necklaces and Aaron took their gold and melted it down over a fire. Then he moulded the gold into the shape of a bull calf, and told the Israelites to worship it.

Aaron had no sooner done this than he grew afraid at what he had done, so he built an altar in front of the calf, and told the people that they must spend the next day worshipping God.

Next morning the people got up early and offered sacrifices before the calf, and worshipped it. Then they began to eat and drink. Before long the whole camp was filled with people dancing and singing and feasting.

Up on the mountain God said to Moses, "Go down at once—your people have done a shameful thing. They have forgotten my commandments and have made themselves a statue of a bull calf. They are kneeling in front of it and making sacrifices, and calling it their god. I shall punish them for this—I shall destroy them all."

"Don't destroy them, Lord," Moses pleaded with him. "Don't be so angry with your own chosen people, whom you took so much trouble to save from Pharaoh. Have mercy—remember Abraham and Isaac and Jacob, and the promise you made them that their children should be as countless as the stars in heaven, and how you promised them their own land for all time."

God listened to Moses, and decided to spare the Israelites after all.

Moses came down from the mountain, carrying the two stone tablets on which God had written all his commandments to the Israelites. Joshua, who was with him, said, "Listen—do you hear all that noise coming from the camp? The people must surely be at war."

"That's not the sound of fighting," Moses replied, "It's the sound of singing and feasting."

When they drew near to the camp they saw the golden calf and the dancing, and Moses was angry—so angry that he flung the tablets down, and they were shattered to pieces at the foot of the mountain. Then he seized the calf and made a great fire and burned it. When the fire had died away Moses took the last remnants of the calf from the fire and ground them to dust. He threw the dust into water and made the people drink it as a punishment.

Moses spoke harshly to Aaron too, but he could see that Aaron was not really able to control the people if he himself was not there. It was on Moses that all the responsibility of leadership always had to rest.

The Renewed Promise

Moses went up Mount Sinai again. "Please show yourself to me in all your glory," he asked God.

"No man can see my face and live," God replied. "But I will put you inside a cleft in the rock and cover you with my hand until I have passed by. Then I will take away my hand and you shall see my back, but my face you must not see.

"Now cut two stone tablets like the ones which you broke, and come to meet me here very early tomorrow morning–but bring no one with you."

So Moses made two more stone tablets, and the next morning very early he climbed Mount Sinai and waited where God had commanded. Then God came down in a cloud of fire and passed in front of him, calling out: "Jehovah the Lord is a merciful God. He forgives those who have done wrong when they ask for forgiveness, but he can punish not only the man who has done wrong, but his children, and his children's children too."

Moses kneeled down and begged God not to punish but to forgive him and his people, and be with them always.

God replied, "I will make a new promise to bind your people and me together. I will perform miracles, I will drive out the tribes who are living in the land I have promised you. Now write down my commandments once again, for they are my covenant–that means my promise to Israel."

Moses stayed on the mountain for 40 more days and nights, and wrote down the words of the promise, which were the Ten Commandments. When at last he had finished, he came down the mountain with the tablets in his arms and the waiting Israelites saw that his face was shining because he had seen the glory of God.

The Departure from Sinai

GOD spoke once again to Moses and said, "It is time now to leave this place and go on to the promised land. I will send an angel ahead of you, and I will drive out the tribes who are living there, as I promised. I will bring you to the land, but I will not come with you myself for I am still angry with your people and in my anger I might destroy them."

When Moses told the people this they felt guilty and sad, and resolved to do better.

They built the tabernacle exactly as God had instructed them, and they put the Ark of the Covenant inside it, in the Holy of Holies, behind the curtain. God covered the tabernacle with a cloud, and accepted it, and made it holy. When the cloud lifted again, the people broke camp and began their journey. God's cloud hung low over the tabernacle by day and was seen as a cloud of fire by night, and it remained with them throughout their journey.

God told Aaron and his sons they were to be his priests, and he gave them this special blessing for the people of Israel:

"May the Lord bless you and keep you; may the Lord make you happy and be good to you; may the Lord look kindly on you and give you peace."

And so, by stages, the Israelites left Sinai and arrived in the wilderness of Paran.

Then came a time when the people began once again to complain about their sufferings. God heard them and grew angry, as he had said he might. He sent a fire that raged through the camp and burned their tents. The people begged Moses to pray for God's forgiveness, and as soon as he did, the fire died down.

But before long the Israelites grew impatient again. "Can't we have meat to eat?" they cried. "In Egypt we had lots of fish, cucumbers and watermelons, leeks and

[86]

onions and garlic. Now there is nothing to eat but this boring manna."

Then God grew angry with them again. He sent them quails to eat for meat, but the meat made them sick, and many of them died.

Aaron and his sister Miriam grew jealous of Moses. "Why should God speak only to Moses?" they said to one another. "Why doesn't he talk to us as well?"

God heard them complaining, and he ordered them to come to his tabernacle.

"My servant Moses is the only one among you I can trust," he said to them. "Because I trust him I can speak to him openly, not in a dream or a vision, as I would talk to an ordinary man. How dare the two of you complain because I talk to your brother alone!"

In his anger God made both Miriam and Aaron ill as a punishment, until Moses once more begged forgiveness for them, and God healed them. Then the people of Israel went wearily on again towards the promised land.

[87]

The Twelve Spies

GOD said to Moses, "I want you to send twelve men ahead to spy out the land of Canaan which I am giving to your people. Pick one man from each tribe to see what life is like there and whether the cities are weakly defended or well fortified."

So Moses chose men of high rank from each tribe, including Joshua the son of Nun. The men made their way up by the Negeb desert to Hebron, and from there up into the hills beyond. They found tribes of tall strong men living there, and many fruit trees, heavy with pomegranates and grapes and figs. They stayed away for 40 days, and when they returned they cut a whole vine branch and brought it back with them, along with baskets of figs and pomegranates, to show their fellow countrymen.

The Israelites gathered around and asked them eagerly about the land of Canaan.

"We made our way into the land, as you told us to," the spies reported to Moses. "It is a rich land, as you can see by the fruit that we have brought back. But its cities are well fortified and there are large numbers of tribes living there already, who have plenty of strong warriors."

Then one of the spies' leaders, a man called Caleb, spoke directly to Moses. "I think that we should advance at once and enter Canaan," he said. "I am sure, with God's help, we are strong enough to conquer it."

But the others disagreed with him. "The men living in Canaan are giants," they insisted. "We are afraid to go there with our families because the people who live there are so tall and strong that we felt like grass-hoppers compared to them. We cannot possibly attack these men—they are far stronger than we are."

When the Israelites heard this, they were angry with Moses and Aaron.

"If only we had died in Egypt or in the wilderness!" they complained. "Why should God bring us all the way here just to die in battle against the fierce men of Canaan?"

And they even talked of finding someone to lead them back to Egypt again.

Two of the spies who had been to Canaan, Joshua and the man named Caleb, tried to rally the people to God's purpose again. "The land we explored is very good indeed," they assured them. "If God is with us he will make it ours. If we only have enough faith in him, he will see that we possess it in the end."

The Israelites paid no attention to them; they just went on shouting at Moses and Aaron.

But God had heard the Israelites' complaints, and he had had enough of them. "I am going to punish your people for having no faith in me," he told Moses. "Not one of you shall see the country I promised to your forefathers, except Joshua and Caleb, who have shown their belief in me. Tomorrow the people must turn back and set out for the wilderness once more. Forty days were spent in exploring Canaan. Now they must wander in the wilderness for 40 years—one year for each of those days—until every last one of them dies there. Only their children will see the promised land. Then I will lead them out of the wilderness at last, and into the land of Canaan."

The King of Edom

THE people of Israel now found themselves on the borders of the kingdom
of Edom. But Moses was afraid to get
into a fight by crossing the land without its
king's permission. So he sent a messenger
to the king of Edom with this message:

"We ask you to allow us to cross from
one side of your country to the other. We
promise we will not trespass on your fields
or vineyards, or drink from your wells without paying."

But the king of Edom refused, and sent
his army to the frontier to stop them entering
his country. The Israelites had to take the
long way around it after all, back into the
wilderness. As usual they were impatient
with Moses, and kept on grumbling and
complaining until God grew so angry that

he sent poisonous snakes among them, so
that many of them were bitten and died.
Realizing they had sinned, the people begged
Moses to ask God's forgiveness.

So Moses pleaded with God, who told
him to make a serpent out of bronze and
hold it up as a standard, so that anyone who
had been bitten by a snake could look at it
and recover.

Then they came to the kingdom of the
Amorites. Here again Moses sent a messenger to the king asking him to let them
pass safely through his land. But the king
refused, and sent the Amorites out to attack
the people of Israel. The Israelites fought
back, so successfully that they defeated the
Amorites and were able to settle in their
land for a while and rest.

King Balek and Balaam, the Holy Man

GOING on their way again, the Israelites arrived in the lowlands of Moab, along the bank of the river Jordan, and camped there.

When Balek, the king of Moab, heard of their arrival he was terrified. There were a lot of Israelites and they had proved that they could defeat the entire Amorite army in battle. King Balek was afraid they would take everything he had. So he sent two of his most trustworthy elders to ask the help of a holy man from Midian named Balaam. The elders travelled to the village where Balaam lived and told him the king had sent for him urgently.

"A whole nation of people has come from Egypt—there are so many of them that they cover the whole country. You must come at once and lay a curse on them before they settle down at our door and take our land away from us."

Balaam listened to them carefully. Then he said, "Spend this night here, and I will see what God wants me to do."

That night God came to Balaam in a dream and said to him, "You are not to curse these people, the Israelites, for they are to be blessed. You may go with these men to King Balek, but you must do what I tell you."

So Balaam saddled his donkey and set out with the Moabite elders.

Balaam and the Angel

GOD was angry because he did not really want Balaam to go, and he sent an angel to bar the path with a sword as Balaam rode on his way.

When Balaam's donkey saw the angel standing in the road, it turned and ran into the fields. Balaam beat the donkey and forced it into a hollow with fenced vineyards on either side. Again the angel appeared in front of them, and the donkey pressed against the fence in fear, so hard that Balaam's foot was painfully crushed between the stirrup and the fence. So he beat the donkey again.

Then the angel of God moved ahead, and stood where the road was so narrow there was no room to turn right or left. The donkey promptly lay down under Balaam and refused to move. Balaam was furious and belaboured the donkey with a stick. But it still refused to move.

Then God gave the donkey the power to speak.

"This is the third time you've beaten me," it said to Balaam. "What have I done wrong?"

"You've made a fool of me," answered the angry Balaam. "Not I," said the donkey. "You've ridden me for years—you know I wouldn't do such a thing."

Then God opened Balaam's eyes and he too saw the angel standing in the road with his sword drawn. He fell to his knees at once, and the angel said to him:

"What do you mean by beating your poor

donkey like that? If it had not seen me and turned aside I would certainly have killed you."

"I have done wrong," Balaam replied. "Do you want me to turn back?"

"No," said the angel. "Go on and meet King Balek. But remember to do as God tells you."

King Balek was greatly relieved when he heard that Balaam was coming, for he still hoped that together they could lay a curse on the Israelites and drive them from the land.

But Balaam warned the king, "I have no power to say or do anything that is against God's will."

Twice King Balek built altars and offered sacrifices of bulls and rams, and twice he commanded Balaam to curse Israel. But each time the old man replied: "God has commanded me to bless Israel, not curse it!"

Then King Balek led Balaam up to a hill where he could see the Israelites encamped in the country beyond.

"Curse them!" he begged. Then the spirit of God filled the old man, and he spoke a prophecy that made King Balek give up:
"How splendid are your tents, O Israel;
  How good is the place where you lie—
  Like long rows of palms,
  Like gardens by a river,
  Like fruit trees that God has planted,
  Like cedars beside the water!
  What its curved horns are to a wild bull,
  God is to you, the nation he brought out
    of Egypt.
  You shall eat up all your enemies,
  Crunch their bones,
  And no one will dare interfere with you.
  A star shall come out of your nation,
  A comet shall arise from Israel
  And do great deeds."

The Death of Moses

GOD said to Moses, "The time of your death is drawing near. Call Joshua and come and stand in front of me in the tabernacle that you have built, so that I can make him your successor."

Then Moses and Joshua went into the tabernacle, and God appeared to them in a pillar of cloud, and the cloud also covered the entrance to the tabernacle, hiding them completely from the watching crowds of Israelites. God said to Moses:

"You are about to die like your fathers, and these people you have led out of Egypt will fall into evil ways. They will worship other gods. They will turn away from me and break my commandments. I shall be angry with them, and I shall leave them to perish when times are hard.

"Now write down my words, so that the Israelites can read them in the days to come and understand why it is that they must suffer these hardships. For the time will come when they will live happily in the land that I promised their forefathers Abraham and Isaac. They will have plenty to eat and to grow—yet they will forget me and turn to other gods instead. Then disasters will overtake them and I will make them suffer for their sins of wrongdoing and lack of faith."

Then God called Joshua the son of Nun to him and said, "Be strong, be firm and purposeful, for it is up to you to bring the people of Israel into the land I have sworn to give them. I am your God and I will always be with you and help you."

Moses wrote down everything God had said to him in a book, which he placed next to the Ark of the Covenant in the tabernacle.

[94]

Then he went out to the waiting people and told them what God had said, warning them solemnly how important it was to obey God's laws. Then he blessed each one of the twelve tribes of Israel in turn, and praised God.

"Praise the Lord you heavens,
  Bow down all you gods, before him.
  For the Lord will give his people justice.
  And have mercy on his chosen servants.
  He will say
  There is no god but me."
That same day God spoke again to Moses,

and said, "Go up onto Mount Nebo in Moab, to the east of Jericho, and look out over the land of Canaan that I am giving to the people of Israel for all time. Look down on its valleys and plains, on its cities, its rivers and its seas. I shall let you see the promised land with your own eyes, but you shall not enter it, because you will die on the mountain and join your forefathers, Abraham and Isaac and Jacob."

Moses made his preparations to go up onto the mountain. He laid his hands on Joshua's shoulders and blessed him as his successor, and Joshua was filled with the wisdom and the truth of God.

Then Moses made his last climb to follow the commands of God. He was old now, after all the years of wandering in the desert, but his eyes were just as clear and his strength just as great as they had always been. Alone he climbed to the top of Mount Nebo, as God had told him to to, and sat with his staff in his hand, looking out over the land of Canaan which stretched far and wide below him. And there he died, as God had said he would.

His body was buried in a valley in Moab—nobody knows where. And all the people of Israel mourned for the man who had been their leader for so long, and wept bitterly.

The Entry into Canaan

AFTER Moses had died, God said to Joshua:

"Now is the time for you to leave the wilderness and cross the river Jordan into the promised land. Everywhere you go will be yours; I am giving it to you, as I promised Moses I would. From the desert to the river Euphrates, and onwards to the Mediterranean Sea shall be your land. No one will ever be able to stand against you; be strong and full of courage, and above all—obey my commandments. If you obey me, I will protect you wherever you go."

Joshua called the people together to tell them what God had said. The Israelites who had left Egypt with Moses had been too impatient to satisfy their hunger and thirst to remember to obey God's commands. But now not one of them was left, except Caleb and Joshua himself, and the men and women who crowded around him had been born during the 40 years of wandering in the wilderness, and had never known slavery. As a result, they were fearless and strong, and full of respect for God and for their leader.

"Whatever you tell us, we will do," they shouted, when Joshua had finished speaking.

"Wherever you send us, we will go!"

Then Joshua said to them, "In three days' time we will cross the river Jordan. Twelve men from the tribes of Israel, one from each tribe, will lead you. The priests will walk in front of you, carrying the Ark of the Covenant of God, and the river will dry up to let you pass."

On the third day the people gathered together on a hill, and the priests and the twelve men, one from each tribe, began carrying the Ark down to the water's edge. When they reached it, Joshua held up Moses' staff, and the priests and the twelve men moved forward. As their feet touched the water, the water piled up into a great wall on either side and the priests were able to step down into the dry river bed. When they reached the middle of the Jordan the priests stood still and lifted the Ark up high, for everyone to see. Meanwhile, each of the twelve men chose a large stone from the middle of the river bed, carried it across to the far side, and set it up there as a memorial to God.

At a sign from Joshua the people of Israel surged forward and crossed the river Jordan, shouting and singing to God as they went. When the last man had crossed to the other side Joshua commanded the priests carrying the Ark to follow on. Slowly they marched to the other side. When they too were on high ground the waters closed up behind them, and the river flowed on as before.

That night the Israelites camped at Gilgal, and celebrated the feast of the Passover. They baked unleavened bread, collecting the wheat from the fields around them, and grinding it into flour. From that day on the manna from heaven stopped, and they ate the food they gathered from the land.

The Fall of Jericho

THE Israelites stayed at Gilgal in Canaan, resting, until they were ready to move westwards to the great city of Jericho. But the people of Jericho were afraid of the Israelites and the power of their God, and bolted every gate into the city.

"I want you to find some way of getting into the city secretly," Joshua said to two of his spies, "and report back everything you see to me."

So the spies searched all around the walls of the fortress, until they found a hidden door. A woman called Rahab saw them there and recognized them as Israelites.

"The people of Jericho are terrified of you," she told them, "because they know you want to attack their city and kill everyone in it. But if you promise to spare me and my family I will help you."

The spies promised Rahab and she let them into the city.

The men looked around them. "It's more like a fortress than a city," one of them remarked, noting the massive walls and the towers manned by well-armed soldiers.

"Yes, and judging by those sacks of wheat and meal they're prepared for a long siege," replied the other.

When the two spies had seen all they wanted, Rahab let them out the same way as they had come and they returned to Joshua.

But Joshua was still not clear in his mind how he and his small band of badly-armed men could storm such a great fortification. He climbed a hill overlooking the city and stood there alone, trying to prepare a plan of attack. Suddenly a man appeared before him, holding a drawn sword in his hand.

"Are you on our side or on our enemy's?" Joshua asked the stranger, and the man replied:

"I am here as captain of the army of our Lord. Take off your sandals; you are standing on holy ground." Joshua fell on his knees at once, and God spoke these words through his angel:

"This is how I shall deliver Jericho and her king into your hands. You must march once around the city with all your warriors, every day for six days, with the Ark of the Covenant carried in front of you. Seven priests blowing trumpets made from rams' horns will march in front of the Ark. On the seventh day you must march around the city seven times, and then the priests will blow their trumpets. This will be the signal for your whole army to shout. Shout, my people, as loud as you can, and the roar of your voices will knock down the city's walls."

Every day for six days the priests and the soldiers marched around the city in silence, carrying the Ark and blowing their trumpets. On the seventh day all the people of Israel joined the march, circling the city seven times. The priests blew their trumpets and then Joshua gave the word. The people let out a great shout. The earth rumbled and shook, and the walls of the city trembled. Then they split right open and crumbled into dust at the feet of the Israelites.

They walked over the remains of the walls into the city and destroyed every single thing in it—except Rahab and her family. The spies were true to their promise that their lives should be spared, and the family settled down among the Israelites.

Joshua Conquers Canaan

JOSHUA and the people of Israel still had a long way to go before the land of Canaan was theirs. There were many fierce battles to fight, for the Hittites and the other tribes living around them hated the Israelites more than anyone.

Joshua decided that one of the first places he would conquer was the city of Ai. He worked out a plan of ambush: most of his men would hide, while he took a handful of them and pretended to attack the city. As he expected, the men of Ai came rushing out to chase the Israelites back into the hills. They left their city undefended behind them while they gave chase, with its gates wide

open. Then Joshua gave the signal for the rest of his army to leave their ambush, and they poured into the deserted city from all sides, and captured it.

The next place Joshua decided to conquer was Gibeon. Here the people were more cunning: they disguised some of their leaders as ambassadors from a distant country, who persuaded Joshua to sign a peace treaty with them. So he signed the treaty and promised that none of his people should harm them. When he found out who the Gibeonites really were, he was angry at their trick. But since he had given his promise not to harm them he punished them

by making them slaves instead, who chopped wood and fetched water to help the Israelites.

When the neighbouring tribes, who were all Amorites, heard how Gibeon had made peace with Joshua, they attacked the city in revenge. But the Gibeonites managed to send a message to Joshua asking him to come and help them. Joshua and his men marched all night and attacked the Amorites unexpectedly, driving them down a steep valley in the hills.

To add to the Amorites' confusion, God sent a terrible storm, with hailstones as big as rocks. Cut down alike by Israelite swords and the gigantic hailstones, the defeated Amorites fled far into the hills, where the Israelites would not bother to follow them. But when the time came to count the dead, more Amorites had been killed by the hailstones than by the Israelite swords.

At last the Israelites could settle down in the lands they had captured and begin to build houses and gardens, and to bring in rich harvests of fruit and grain.

As long as Joshua was alive they kept God's commandments. But after Joshua's death, the Israelites were ruled by the judges, and a new generation of people grew up, who began to worship new gods. "Let's build new statues and dance and drink to them, and make sacrifices to them," they said to one another. And they did all these things. But God was angry with them for breaking his covenant, and decided to teach them a lesson.

The nearest enemy tribe was that of the Canaanites. Their raiding parties were constantly stealing the Israelites' herds and burning and looting their villages. One day, however, their army came in force and defeated the Israelites. Then they captured

every man, woman and child and made them slaves.

The commander of the Canaanite army was a cruel man named Sisera, who hated the Israelites and did everything he could to make their lives as miserable as possible.

For twenty years God allowed this, until the prayers of the unhappy Israelites moved him to set them free. The judge who had been appointed to rule Israel at that time was a woman called Deborah. She was a very wise woman, and God spoke to her.

"Barak," she said to one of the Israelite soldiers, "gather 10,000 men and march to Mount Tabor. I will see that Sisera and all his army are there too. He will fight you and you will defeat him."

When Sisera heard that Barak had gathered an army together he galloped to meet him, with his army and 900 war chariots. But God wanted Barak and Deborah to win, and they

did. The chariots were wrecked, and Sisera's army was completely destroyed.

Sisera himself escaped on foot into the countryside, looking desperately for a place to hide from Barak and his men. At last he came to a tent he recognized. The woman who came out to meet him was the wife of a man who was friendly to his people. Sisera was tired and thirsty. Here, he thought, he would be safe.

The woman, an Israelite whose name was Jael, welcomed him inside the tent. She gave him a drink of goat's milk from the skin she kept inside the tent, and hid him under a rug.

Sisera was tired after the battle, and soon fell asleep. Then Jael took a tent peg and a hammer, and crept up to his sleeping body. She felt for his head under the rug, and when she had found it she drove the peg right into his skull and killed him.

Gideon Defeats the Midianites

IT was a bad time for the people. The Israelites were being threatened by enemy tribes from all sides. The Midianites and the Amalekites came with their fast camels and raided and plundered whatever they could. The Israelites had to hide their food and their possessions, and even threshed their wheat in secret so that it would not be taken away from them.

A young man called Gideon was working near his father's barn, threshing wheat quickly so that he could hide it. Suddenly a voice spoke behind him:

"You are a brave man, and God is with you."

Gideon turned round in surprise. He did not feel brave; he was the youngest son of an unimportant family in a weak tribe, that of Manasseh. Then he saw who it was who had spoken to him. An angel of God was sitting under a tree, looking at him. Rising and coming closer, the angel went on:

"You are a strong man, Gideon. Go and use this strength to free Israel from its enemies."

Gideon shook his head.

"How can I begin such a task?" he said. "I am no leader. And besides, no one would ever listen to me. I am not a good speaker."

The angel persisted. "You can begin here, in your own town of Ophrah. In the market place there is an altar, put up by the people to worship the idol Baal. Get your father's bull and collect a few of your friends together. Go there in the middle of the night and cast ropes around the idol, and let your bull pull it down from the altar. Smash it to pieces."

Gideon was still not sure that this really was a messenger from God. He said:

"My lord, how do I know that God wants me to do this? If I smash the idol the people will be angry with my family, and they may kill us. Can you give me proof that you are sent by God?"

The angel replied, "Go into your house and fetch me the pot of meat from your oven, and some bread."

Gideon did as he was asked, and returned with the food. He put the bread down on a flat stone, and poured the meat from the pot over it.

"Stand back," the angel said, and touched the meat with his staff.

There was a flash of fire, and the food on the stone disappeared, and the angel with it.

Then Gideon knew that the angel was truly God's messenger, and that God would help him. He felt new strength swelling inside him.

That night he went to the market place and pulled down the idol. In the morning, when the people saw what he had done, they wanted to kill him. But his father stopped them.

"If Baal is such a great god," he cried, "let him show his power! Let him come down and kill my son himself!"

So the people started praying and dancing round the broken altar of Baal, calling on their god for revenge. But there was no power in Baal, and Gideon remained free.

The word quickly spread that God had chosen Gideon as the people's new leader.

Men came to him from all the tribes of Israel, ready to fight with him against the Midianites. God helped Gideon choose the bravest among them, and from these he hand-picked the 300 best men. God said to Gideon:

"Go up into the hills above the Midianites' camp. Take these 300 men with you, and tell them each to carry a trumpet and some oil jars. Form a ring above the camp and wait until it is dark."

The men stationed themselves on the hill-

tops and watched the army of Midianites encamped in the plains below. Brave as they were, they could not see how so few of them could destroy this large force. When night fell Gideon gave each man a torch.

"Watch me," he said. "When I set fire with this torch to the oil in my jar, do the same. When I blow on my trumpet you will blow on yours."

At a sign from Gideon, the night was filled with the sound of trumpets from every hill. The men lit their oil jars and threw them into the plains below. They rolled down the slopes like balls of fire, into the camp of the sleeping Midianites. The Midianites awoke in panic and began attacking one another in the dark.

In the confusion many of them killed each other, and when daylight came those who remained alive were no match for Gideon's men. They fought bravely, but God was on the side of Gideon and the Israelites, and soon the Midianite army was completely destroyed.

Jotham and Abimelech

IN one of the smaller kingdoms in Canaan there lived an evil and ambitious man called Abimelech. He was the son of Gideon and of a slave girl and he wanted to be king. There was no reason why he should be, nor had God shown in any way that he wanted him to become a leader.

So Abimelech decided to claim the crown without help from God or man. First he went to his mother's family in Shechem and borrowed money. His uncles gave him 70 pieces of silver. With these he hired 70 men, cut-throats and bandits, who were prepared to do any evil task for the money.

Then Abimelech returned to his father's family, at Ophrah, taking the 70 cut-throats with him.

"Kill my brothers," he told them. "There are 70 of them. Make sure that they are all killed, for I want to be king. I do not want to share my throne with anyone."

Then the cut-throats murdered every one of them except Jotham, the youngest of Abimelech's brothers, who escaped.

At last Abimelech thought the crown was his. He called the people of Shechem together, and proclaimed himself their new king. They cheered him, and were about to lead him to his throne when Jotham appeared on the top of a nearby hill.

"People of Shechem!" he shouted down to them. "You have taken a traitor and a murderer as your leader. A curse on you and on him! This man will destroy the citizens of Shechem, and they will destroy him!" Then he escaped before anyone could take him prisoner.

Three years passed, during which Abimelech ruled the country without any opposition. Then God punished the king for the murder of his brothers.

First, he turned the people of Shechem against Abimelech. They tried to ambush the king and his army, but the attempt failed. Then Abimelech captured the city and pulled down every building in it, strewing the ground with salt so that nothing would ever grow there.

So the people of Shechem were all killed by Abimelech, and the first part of Jotham's curse was fulfilled.

But Abimelech's thirst for power was not satisfied. He captured the cities in the lands around him, and took their people into slavery. One day he attacked the city of Thebez and captured it. In the centre of the city was a castle, where the defenders retreated. As Abimelech came close to the walls to give the order to attack, a woman dropped a millstone on his head, and fractured his skull.

"Quick, I am dying," Abimelech called to his armour bearer. "Do not let people say I was killed by a woman. Kill me with your sword!" So the young man stabbed Abimelech to death with his sword, and the rest of Jotham's curse was fulfilled: Abimelech was killed by one of his own men.

Jephthah's Vow

THE people of Israel still had enemies all around them. They needed someone strong to lead them, and they chose a man named Jephthah.

Jephthah had had a hard childhood. His family had made him leave home because he was only a half-brother, and he had to struggle for himself and make a new life among strangers. He collected a few men around him and trained them to fight. There was something great about him, and people began to notice him.

One day a group of the most important men of Israel came to him and said:

"Jephthah, our country is in great danger. Our enemies, the Ammonites, are massing their armies on our borders. They will attack us at any time. We need you to fight for us, to lead us in battle against them."

Jephthah hesitated. He wasn't sure that he wanted to fight for his people; they had never done anything to make him feel welcome when his own family had thrown him out.

"If you win this war for us, we will make you ruler over all the land," the elders promised. So Jephthah went back with them and was made commander of the army.

Jephthah was a brave man but he realized it would be better not to fight the Ammonites if there was any chance of avoiding it. He sent messengers to the Ammonite king to ask why he wanted to invade the country of Israel. "You have stolen land that rightly belongs to us," the king told them. "Give it

back and then we will leave you in peace."

"We have stolen no land," Jephthah's messengers replied. "We are living in a country that used to belong to the Amorites. It was never yours and we have done you no wrong. You are doing wrong by attacking us. Let us live side by side in peace."

But the Ammonite king paid no attention. He was determined to fight.

Jephthah had trained the Israelite army carefully and was sure they would obey his orders. But he was not sure that he and his men were strong enough to defeat the Ammonites, and so he prayed to God. He made the most solemn oath that he could think of. "If you let me defeat the Ammonites," he said to God, "then I promise to sacrifice to you the first living creature that runs out of my house to greet me on my return!"

Then he led his men into battle against the Ammonites. God gave the Israelites strength, and soon their enemies were fleeing before them. The Israelites pursued them, killing them as they ran. The victory was complete.

After the battle Jephthah returned home. He had not forgotten his promise to God. But when he reached his house, who should be the first living creature to run and meet him? His daughter, his only child! She was

with a group of her friends, laughing and dancing and playing her tambourine.

With terrible sorrow in his heart Jephthah told her what he had sworn to do. She knew he must keep his promise. She said simply:

"Dear father, you have given your word, and you must not break it now. But before you kill me, let me go and roam the hills with my friends for two months so that I may prepare myself to die."

Jephthah let his daughter go, and at the end of two months she returned. Then he offered her as a sacrifice to God, and with her death, his vow was fulfilled.

The Story of Samson

SOMETIMES God chose the least likely men and women to work for him. There was Samson–a rough, wild man with a short temper–who was for ever getting into trouble with his own people, the Israelites, and his enemies, the Philistines.

But he had been marked out by God from the start. Before he was born his mother was visited by an angel.

"You shall have a son," he had said to her, "who will belong to God. He will be marked out from other people by his hair. It will make him as strong as a lion, and for that reason it must never be cut."

God's words came true. The baby was born and the woman named him Samson. He grew into a fine young man, larger and stronger than any around him, and his parents were very proud of him. One day, he told his parents he wanted to marry a

Philistine girl whom he had seen in the neighbouring town of Timnath. They were not pleased because the Philistines were their enemies, but Samson insisted.

As he was walking through the vineyards on his way to Timnath, he was attacked by a lion. He had no weapon, but God gave him the strength to kill the lion with his bare hands. He left the carcass lying there and went on to visit the girl. The marriage was arranged to take place in a few weeks.

At the wedding feast Samson boasted that he would set the guests a riddle that none of them could answer.

"Out of the eater came something to eat,
Out of the strong came something sweet,"
he said. (On the way to the feast he had seen that bees had made a nest inside the carcass of the lion he had killed, and built a honeycomb.)

The guests could not answer the riddle. In the end, tired of guessing, they persuaded his bride to ask him what the answer was. He told her, and in no time at all the girl had disclosed it to the Philistines. They came back to him, shouting:

"What is sweeter than honey?
What is stronger than a lion?"

Samson was so angry at what his wife had done that he killed 30 young men and burned the Philistines' crops in revenge. They in turn killed the treacherous bride and her father. Ill feeling between the two tribes had reached a peak.

Then one day Samson disappeared and

went to live high up in the mountains, in a cave. The Philistines turned on Samson's people and gave them more trouble than ever before. In the end, in return for peace, they forced the people to say where Samson was hiding, and to bring him down from the mountains, tied up with ropes.

When Samson came face to face with his enemies again his old anger returned. He strained at the ropes that held him down, and they snapped like gut strings. He looked around for some weapon, and snatched up the jawbone from a dead donkey lying beside the road. With it he attacked the

Philistines so fiercely that 1,000 men fell dead under his blows, and the rest fled in terror. Still Samson's enemies were determined to capture him. The Philistines knew that they would never catch him by force, for he was stronger than any man. He could tear down doors and break through chains. His strength had been given him by God, and it was this secret power that the Philistines were determined to break.

They went to a beautiful woman named Delilah, and told her to spy on him.

"Find out by what magic means he remains so strong," they said. "If you can make him weak like other men, we will give you 1,100 pieces of silver."

It did not take Delilah long to make Samson come and see her. It took her even less long to make him fall in love with her, and to promise to give her whatever she asked for.

"Tell me the secret of your great strength, Samson," she asked.

"Tie me up with new bow strings, and I will grow weak like other men," he said. So Delilah waited until he was asleep and then tied him up with the strings.

"The Philistines are attacking you, Samson!" she cried.

Samson awoke instantly and freed himself with one quick wrench. Then he stood there laughing at Delilah for pretending to capture him.

She asked him again, "Tell me the secret of your strength, Samson." "Tie me up with new rope, and I will grow weak like other men," he said.

Again she waited until he was asleep, and again she tied him up. "The Philistines are attacking you!" she cried. Samson woke, and broke through the rope as if it had been a thread.

At last he told her the truth. "I am one of the people chosen by God," he said. "My strength lies in my hair; it must never be

cut. If it is, I will become as weak as other men."

Delilah drugged his wine and cradled him to sleep on her lap. Then she cut off his hair. She called in the Philistines and they bound him and blinded him and threw him into prison. They paid Delilah the silver.

Samson was put to work like an animal, grinding grain. Now that he was blind and weak, the Philistines decided to put him on show to the public in the temple. The people crowded into the temple of their god, Dagon, celebrating Samson's downfall. When they saw their old enemy they jeered. "O Lord," Samson prayed to God, "give me back just once more the strength I used to have."

God guided him to the two central pillars that supported the temple. Samson took hold of one pillar with his right arm, and the other with his left. "Let me die with the Philistines," he prayed, and then he heaved at the pillars with all his strength.

The pillars cracked, then they broke, and with a roar like that of an earthquake the whole temple collapsed, burying everyone in it under a heap of stones. The people who mocked Samson were killed, and so was he.

Ruth and Naomi

MANY years ago there lived in Bethlehem a man and a woman and their two sons. They were hard-working, good people, but they were poor, and there was a famine in the land.

"All around us people are starving," Elimelech, the husband, said. "There is no grain left, and even the wells are running dry. We must find somewhere better, another country where the harvests are good and there is plenty of food."

So Elimelech and Naomi his wife took their two sons and crossed the Dead Sea to the land of Moab on its eastern shore. The

harvests had been better there and the people had enough to eat. So instead of sending the strangers away with harsh words, the Moabites made them welcome and helped them to find a house and settle down.

The family worked hard and in time both the sons were old enough to get married. Their wives were Moabite women from the village where they lived. One of the girls was named Orpah, and the other Ruth.

Then one day Elimelech died. While Naomi was mourning her husband's death she had an even greater loss. Her two sons, young and strong as they were, fell ill and

died too. The three women were left alone, helpless.

"Your husbands are dead," Naomi said to the two girls, "and I am old and a foreigner in your country. Go and find yourselves new husbands who will look after you. Go, while you are still young and beautiful. Marry and have children. I will return alone to my own country, to mourn the death of my three men."

The girls did not want to leave Naomi, whom they loved. But at last she persuaded Orphah to return to her family and find a new husband in the land of Moab. Naomi's other daughter-in-law, Ruth, clung to her and said:

"I will always stay with you. I do not want to go back to my parents' people, nor worship their gods again. I will go with you wherever you go, and will stay with you wherever you stay. Your people shall be my people and your God my God. Where you die I will die, and where you are buried I will be buried. I swear by your God that nothing but death shall divide us."

Naomi was moved by her daughter-in-law's words and together they set out from Moab across the Dead Sea to return to Bethlehem.

When they arrived in Bethlehem the whole town welcomed them, and the women who had known Naomi before she left said to her:

"Can this be Naomi, our friend? How is your husband and how are your two fine sons?"

"Do not call me Naomi now," she replied. "Call me Mara, which means bitter. I no longer have a husband, and my two fine sons are dead."

"But you still have a daughter," Ruth reminded her, and kissed her.

[115]

Ruth and Boaz

It was harvest time and the fields around Bethlehem were heavy with grain. "Go and pick up grain in the field that belongs to Boaz," Naomi said to Ruth. "He was related to my dead husband, and he is a kind man and will let you glean the wheat his reapers have left."

So Ruth went out to the wheatfields. Slowly the rows of reapers moved forward across the fields, cutting the wheat with sickles and tying the stalks into sheaves. Behind them followed the gleaners—women like Ruth who collected the stray ears of wheat the reapers dropped. It was backbreaking work, for they had to bend low to see the husks of wheat lying on the ground,

and it would take them all day to fill a small sack. But in this way people who had no fields of their own could get enough wheat to grind into flour and make bread for their families.

As the sun rose higher in the sky Boaz came out into the field, and watched the harvesters at work. He greeted them.

"The Lord be with you," he said, and they replied, "The Lord bless you." Then he noticed Ruth among the gleaners.

"Who is that girl?" he asked.

"She is a Moabite," his men replied. "She came here from her own country to be with the widow Naomi, your cousin. She has been on her feet since sunrise, gathering the

corn without stopping to rest at all."

Boaz called Ruth to him. "Stay in my field until the harvest is over," he said. She thanked him. "Stay and drink with us," Boaz went on. "I will see that no man bothers you. If you are thirsty, drink from my jars."

Ruth thanked him again and said, "Why are you so kind to me? I am a foreigner here." And Boaz replied:

"I have heard of your faithfulness and your love for Naomi. The God of Israel will bless you for it." Then he invited her to sit with him among the reapers and eat bread with him, and dip the bread in his wine. He gave her roasted grain to eat and she ate all she needed and saved the rest for Naomi. Boaz gave orders that she should be allowed to collect as much of his barley and wheat as she wished, even from among the sheaves.

The summer passed. The harvest had been gathered in, and the harvest festival had begun. Naomi said to her daughter-in-law:

"Tonight Boaz is threshing barley in his barn. He is my cousin, and, according to our laws, he can take you into his house as his wife. Go to him tonight; perhaps he will help you."

Ruth did as Naomi suggested, and Boaz greeted her joyfully, because he already loved her. He wanted to marry her, but he had to ask a cousin more closely related to the family than he was for permission. The cousin gave his consent and, as was customary, he showed his agreement by taking off his sandal and giving it to Boaz.

So Ruth became Boaz's wife and bore him a son. And Naomi's house was filled with children again by the daughter-in-law who loved her so dearly.

Samuel, Child of the Lord

THERE were two Israelite women married to the same husband: Peninnah, who had children, and Hannah, who had none. Every day Hannah would pray to God to give her a child, and every day Peninnah would mock her because he did not. When their husband, Elkanah, went to the temple of God to offer sacrifices, Hannah went with him to beg God for a son.

"Lord, please let me have a child," she prayed. "If you give me a son, then he shall be yours. I swear that I will bring him back to this temple, to serve you as one of your priests."

God heard her prayer. He gave her the son she longed for, and she called the boy Samuel. Much as she loved him, she remembered her promise. When he was not yet two years old, she went with Elkanah to the temple and brought Samuel to the priest, an old man called Eli. "This is my son whom God has given me," she said. "Now I am lending him back to God; his whole life shall be spent in God's service."

The boy Samuel grew up in the temple, where he was taught and cared for by Eli, who loved him like his own son.

One night, while Samuel was asleep, he heard a voice call, "Samuel, Samuel." He went to Eli and said, "Here I am."

"I did not call you," Eli replied.

Samuel went back to bed. But again the voice called, "Samuel, Samuel," and again he went to Eli. "Here I am," he said. "Surely you called me."

"I did not call you, my son," Eli replied. "Lie down again."

When Samuel was summoned for the third time Eli understood that it was God who was calling the child. "If he calls again," the priest said to Samuel, "you must say, 'Speak, Lord, your servant is listening.'"

Samuel went back to his place in the temple. "Samuel, Samuel!" the voice of God called once more, and this time Samuel replied, "Speak, Lord, your servant is listening."

Then the temple was filled with God's presence, and from that day on Samuel became God's prophet as Moses had been, and told the Israelites what God wanted them to do.

The years went by. The Israelites went to war with the Philistines again and the Philistine army won one battle after another. In desperation the Israelites sent men to fetch the Ark of the Covenant from God's temple, hoping that its presence would bring their army new strength. But God was angry with the Israelites for worshipping other gods, and allowed the battle to go against them.

The Philistines attacked so vigorously

that they broke right through the Israelite lines and captured the sacred Ark. Demoralized, the Israelite army turned and fled.

When the old priest Eli heard that the Ark was captured, he was so distressed that he collapsed and died. Samuel was appointed Israel's leader and judge in his place.

The Ark did not stay long in the hands of the Philistines, however. They moved it from one city to another, but wherever it was kept the people fell sick and died, and the cities swarmed with rats.

So the Philistines returned the Ark to the Israelites, with rich gifts, and made peace with them. Samuel ruled Israel justly and the people worshipped God again.

Samuel and Saul

WHEN Samuel was an old man the Israelite leaders came to him one day as he was sitting in the judge's seat in Ramah, the town where he lived.

"You are nearly blind, Samuel," they said to him, "and your work is growing too much for you. What we want is a king. Not just a judge over Israel, like you, but a real king with absolute power over everything."

"God is your king," said Samuel.

"We have many gods, not just your one," the people replied, "and now we want a king to lead us in battle. Maybe we'll have less trouble from our enemies then."

When God heard how the people talked he resolved to teach them a lesson. "I will send them a king," he told Samuel, "who will make them suffer. He will take their sons and make them fight for him. He will take their harvest and their fields, and make them his own. He will take their daughters and make them his slaves. They will regret that they ever asked him to be king." Samuel told the people what God had said. But they did not listen to him.

God chose a man to be king who was the complete opposite to Samuel. His name was Saul. He was young and strong, good-looking and tall, and he came from a wealthy family. Wherever he went he stood out in a crowd, for he was a head taller than anyone else. He was not as wise nor as good as Samuel but he suited God's purpose for the moment.

Saul's father, like most other people at that time, had his own herd of cattle. One

day his donkeys broke loose and strayed out of the neighbourhood.

"Go and look for them," Saul's father said to him, "and take one of the servants with you."

Saul searched for them in the cornfields, the vineyards and the olive groves. He went further and further afield, but he could not find them. He knew that if he stayed away much longer his father would begin to worry about him.

"Come, let's go back," he said to his servant. But the servant replied:

"A man of God lives near here. He is a prophet, and everything he says about the future is true because God speaks to him. Maybe he can tell us where our donkeys are."

So they set off to the nearby town to find Samuel.

The old man was just coming out of the town gates on his way to pray at the altar on the nearby hill. God had already told him

that the man who was to be king would come to him that day. As Saul came towards Samuel, God spoke to his prophet again.

"This is the man I want to be king," he said. "This man shall rule my people."

So Samuel welcomed Saul warmly. "I am the man you are looking for," he said. "Don't worry any more about your donkeys. They are safe. Come and stay at my house tonight and I will tell you God's plans for you."

Saul Is Chosen King

SAUL was made king in a simple, profound ceremony that kings have followed through the ages. His head was anointed with oil. Samuel, the old, blind prophet who was handing over some of his power to Saul, took a small flask of holy oil and poured it over the young man's head. Then he kissed him and said:

"The Lord has anointed you to rule his people, and to deliver them from their enemies."

He sent Saul to the hill of God, to offer sacrifices and pray. On the way there Saul met a band of holy men coming down from the altar at the top of the hill. They were playing the lute, the harp, the pipe and the drum, and their music filled Saul with the spirit of God, like a prophet.

When the people saw him like this they said, "What has happened to Saul? Can this be the same man we have always known? Is Saul now one of the prophets?" From that day on Saul was a new man, because he had seen some of the beauty of God.

Meanwhile Samuel called together all the tribes of Israel. He said to them:

"You have rejected your God, and have asked me to find a king in his place. Your king is here. He is Saul, chosen for you by God."

When the people saw the young and handsome man they shouted:

"Long live the king!" because they were well pleased with him.

So Saul became king and fought many battles against the Philistines.

[122]

Jonathan Breaks an Oath

TIME passed and Saul's eldest son Jonathan grew into a fine soldier, and joined his father in fighting the Philistines. They had established a stronghold in the hills, and Saul's army was encamped facing it on the other side of a deep ravine. Jonathan looked at the great rock face and said to his armour bearer:

"We will climb this rock and attack the Philistines from the front."

The Philistines meanwhile had sent out raiding parties to attack Saul's defences from behind. They had left their own post overlooking the ravine almost unguarded.

Jonathan and his armour bearer scrambled up the steep cliff. When they appeared in front of the Philistine outpost the few men left there fled in panic. The Philistine soldiers started fighting each other in confusion. Then Saul crossed the ravine with his men and routed the whole Philistine army.

Saul vowed to God that no man in his army was to eat until dusk, when there would be a general thanksgiving. But Jonathan did not know about his father's oath. He was pursuing the Philistines through a wood when he came across some wild honey in a tree trunk and ate it.

"We owe him our victory. Do not kill him for breaking the oath!" the people pleaded with Saul, and they ransomed Jonathan's life instead.

[123]

Saul Disobeys God

WHEN Saul was king of Israel there seemed to be one war after another. The most feared of the Israelites' enemies were the Amalekites. Ever since the time when the Amalekites had attacked the Israelites in the desert on their way from Egypt, there had been wars between the two nations.

God said to Samuel, "Go to King Saul and tell him to arm his men. The time has come for every one of the Amalekites and all their possessions to be destroyed. Spare no one; I want every man and every beast killed."

When Samuel had told Saul of God's command, he gathered his troops together and prepared to attack. The battle that followed was fierce and long, and almost all the Amalekites were killed in it.

When they saw that they were victorious, Saul's men were filled with greed for the Amalekites' possessions. Against God's command they rounded up the cattle and kept what was best in the land. Saul did nothing to stop them.

God was angry, and sent Samuel to tell Saul he had done wrong. Saul begged for forgiveness – the animals, he said, were intended to be sacrificed to God.

"God wants obedience more than sacrifices," Samuel told him. "He rejects you as king of Israel."

As Samuel turned to go, Saul caught at his robe to stop him, but it tore in his hands. Samuel turned round. "God will tear the kingdom of Israel away from you and give it to a better man," he said to Saul. And then he left. He would never see Saul again.

David, Son of Jesse

David, Son of Jesse

THE prophet Samuel was sad because Saul, the king he had anointed, had angered God and been rejected as king. He was worried, too, because the Israelites could not survive as a nation if they did not have a strong leader.

Then God spoke to Samuel as he sat in his garden, and told him his new plans.

"Go to Bethlehem, Samuel," God said, "to the house of a man called Jesse. I have chosen one of his sons to be the new king. I will tell you which one I want, and you will anoint him as king."

"But Lord," Samuel protested, "Saul is a man who is quick to get angry, and violent when he is in a rage. When he hears what I have done he will try to kill me."

"Don't be afraid," God said to him. "Take a calf with you and tell the people you have come there to sacrifice it to me."

So Samuel made his way to Bethlehem. When he came near to the city the elders came out to meet him.

"Why are you here? Is everything all right?" they asked, and Samuel replied, "I have come to offer a sacrifice to God."

Then he sent to Jesse, who was the grandson of Ruth and Boaz, and said:

"Bring your sons to the sacrifice, and let them stand before me."

Jesse and his sons washed themselves and put on clean clothes in preparation for the sacred service. As they came up to the priest, Samuel blessed them. Then he said:

"Come, Jesse, show me your sons."

Jesse called his eldest son, Eliab, and presented him to Samuel. "This is a fine young man," thought Samuel, but God gave him no sign. So the prophet bowed his

head, and Eliab moved on. Then Jesse called his second son, Abinadab, and Shammah, his third. Seven sons of Jesse were presented to Samuel, and seven times he bowed his head. Each time the prophet said:

"Is there another son of Jesse?"

Finally Jesse said, "There is one more; the youngest, who is minding the sheep. His name is David."

"Send for him," the prophet said. When David came Samuel saw that he was a handsome boy, and that his eyes were bright. Then God said to the prophet:

"Rise up and anoint him; this boy shall be king."

Samuel rose and took the flask filled with holy oil from his side. He held it high, and poured the oil over David's head, and anointed him as king. Then the spirit of God filled the boy, and remained with him from that day onwards.

Meanwhile a sickness had clouded the mind of King Saul. He would be seized by sudden fits of fierce anger and terrible sadness.

"Your mind is burning," his men said to him. "Some music would soothe and cool your fever."

"Where can such music be found?" the king asked. "I know a boy, David the son of Jesse, who plays the harp," said one of his men. "I am sure his music cannot fail to heal you."

So Saul sent for the shepherd boy. David came, bringing gifts from his father for the king. Then he sat down beside him, and played the harp and sang. The king was comforted by his music and grew well again.

David and Goliath

THE Philistines were on the move again. David was too young to fight in King Saul's army so he went on minding his father's sheep. But he longed to be a soldier like his three eldest brothers, who were fighting with the king.

David was sitting at table with his father Jesse, one day, when Jesse said to him:

"I want you to take this food to your brothers and then come back and tell me how they are."

David wasted no time. He found someone to look after the sheep in his place, and set off early the next morning. He reached King Saul's camp just as the two great armies were preparing themselves for the battle. The war cries of the Israelites, and the answering cries of their enemy, the Philistines, beat on his ears like fists on a drum.

There was no sign of his brothers in the rear column of soldiers, where David first looked. He pushed through the crowd of shouting soldiers until he found his brothers in the front line, near the king.

"What are you doing here?" Eliab, the eldest, cried when he saw David. "Go back at once; this is no place for a boy!"

Before David could reply there was a

sudden silence. From among the ranks of the Philistine army a giant, Goliath, had appeared.

"I challenge you, men of Israel," he roared. "If any one of you defeats me single-handed, we Philistines will be your slaves. If your man loses, we will take you all! Who among you is brave enough to fight me?"

"I am," shouted David.

The whole army of Israel turned to look at the boy, and his brothers said, "David, go home at once and mind your sheep."

David pushed his way forward to the king.

"Let me fight Goliath, sir," he begged, "and I will bring victory to Israel."

"You are a boy," the king said to him. "You cannot fight a giant like Goliath!"

"I am a shepherd," David replied. "When wild animals come and attack my father's flock I kill them. I have killed lions and bears, and I can kill Goliath—I know I can!"

"Go, then," said Saul, "and God be with you."

Saul put a bronze helmet on David's head and gave him a coat of mail to wear. Then he handed the boy his own sword.

David hesitated. "I cannot fight with these on," he said. "I must be free." He took off the king's armour again, and picked up his sling. Then he chose five smooth stones and put them in his shepherd's pouch.

The men around him fell back as he advanced, bare-handed, towards the giant Philistine, who stood towering above the armour bearer who carried his shield.

"I am ready," he said.

Goliath looked at his opponent. "You?" he said. "Who are you?" He fingered the sword he was carrying. A dagger hung from his belt, and he held a spear in his right hand. "I will take you and cut you up, and throw you to the sparrows as food," he said.

David moved forwards. "I am David, the son of Jesse," he said. "The men you see before you are soldiers of the army of our

Lord. Through our victory over the Philistines the world will know that our God is the true God, and that there is no other god than he. I am going to fight you and kill you, Goliath!"

With these words David raised his sling and aimed the stone in it at the giant. The stone flew through the air. It struck Goliath on the forehead, and the huge Philistine crashed to the ground. David ran to him and drew his sword out of its sheath. He held it high, and then sliced downwards, cutting off Goliath's head.

That was how the boy David became a hero in a day by killing the giant Goliath.

Saul's Jealousy

FROM the day that David killed Goliath his life changed completely. King Saul brought him to live in the palace and treated him like a son. Jonathan loved David like a brother and the two young men did everything together. From being a shepherd David became a soldier. Like Jonathan, he was given an army to command, and with it he won every battle against the Philistines.

People began to make up songs about David. He became so popular that everything he did was set to music. One day the king heard a woman singing, and asked what the words of the song were. He was told:

"One thousand men have fallen to Saul; *Ten* thousand men to David."

Just then Saul saw David return, leading the army home from another great victory over the Philistines. The people lined the streets, cheering and waving. That was enough to make the king fall into a fit of jealousy.

"They will make him king next!" he muttered. Then he added, "But I will kill him first!"

As he had done so often before, he called David to play the harp to him. In the past the beautiful music of the instrument had soothed the king and kept him sane. But

now David's skill with it only increased the king's jealousy. Something seemed to snap inside his head, and he hurled his spear at David. Swift as a leopard, David swerved aside.

Saul's fits of insanity grew worse. With every battle that David won, his jealousy increased. Finally David had to flee for his life, into the hills of Ziph.

Saul set out in person to hunt him down. There seemed no escape for David; the king's men were all around. But just then Saul was diverted by the Philistines, who attacked him from behind. This gave David the chance to escape deeper into the hills, to a place called Engedi. Here King Saul picked up his trail again.

David and his men had hidden themselves in a cave when, by chance, the king came into it, alone and undefended.

"This is your chance, sir," David's men whispered to him. "Quick! Kill him while he is here!"

"I cannot kill Saul," David replied. "He is my king; God has anointed him to lead me."

Instead, he cut off a piece of the king's cloak, and when Saul left the cave he followed him and called after him:

"My lord the king!"

Saul looked round and saw David kneeling in front of the cave.

"Why do you fear me, sir?" David asked. "Look, here is a piece of your cloak that I cut off while you were in my power inside the cave. I could have killed you, but I didn't, for you are my king, the king of all Israel."

Then Saul was moved with love for David again, and his madness left him.

David Marries Saul's Daughter

SAMUEL the prophet died and all the Israelites gathered to mourn for him. Saul and David attended the ceremony as friends. But it was not long before Saul's madness returned. However much loyalty David showed his king, the fear remained with Saul that he would kill him. The fact that everyone loved David – the soldiers, the people, the king's son Jonathan – Saul could see only as a plot by David to take the throne from him.

Saul had failed to kill David with his own hands. Now he planned that the Philistines should do it for him. He knew that his daughter Michal was in love with David and that he, as a humble shepherd's son, could not expect to marry into the king's family. Saul resolved to use Michal as a bait to lure David to his death.

He sent for David and said to him:

"I will give you Michal in marriage if you can buy her from me. Her price is high. You yourself must kill 100 Philistines in battle."

David was not afraid of the Philistines, and he wanted to marry Michal. He said to Saul:

"Your offer is fair. I accept the bargain."

He did not have to wait long. The Philistines attacked the borders of Israel, and

David's men went out to meet them. Once more David won the battle; by the end of the day 200 Philistines lay dead in the field. David came back triumphantly to Saul.

"I have killed double the number of Philistines you set as your price," he said. "Now give Michal to me in marriage." So, instead of having David killed by the Philistines, Saul had to make him his son-in-law.

But his obsession never left him. He grew more and more afraid of David and was convinced that David meant to murder him. He

called his guards together and told them, "Go to David's house and surround it. Before daylight, I want you to break in and kill him."

When Michal caught sight of her father's men massing around their house, she said to David:

"My father has sent his men to murder you! I know a secret window through which you can escape. I will pretend to the murderers that you are still here in order to give you time to get clear of the city." She hurried to David's bed and filled it with pillows so that it looked as if a man was sleeping in it. Then she put a goatskin where his head should be, and drew the curtains across the windows to dim the light in the room. Then she took David to the secret window and let him down outside the city wall on a rope, so that he could escape into the hills.

At dawn, Saul's men broke into the house. They lifted the bed with the dummy in it and carried it to the king. When Saul saw that David had once again escaped, the madness in him rose to a fury.

David and Jonathan

spoken for him. "You have no cause to fear David," Jonathan told his father. "We have exchanged oaths of friendship with each other. I have given him my cloak, my sword, my bow and my belt as tokens of my love for him. He will never do you harm."

ALTHOUGH Saul was so angry with David, the king's son Jonathan remained his friend. Jonathan was graceful and swift, famed for his skill with the bow. As a huntsman he was second to none. David was fearless. He could lead men to victory and then sing and make music about it afterwards. This is one of his songs:

"It is good to give thanks to God,
Because his love will last for ever.
If we break his commandments,
We are lost in darkness like prisoners
Bound in chains.
Our spirits are broken by hard work,
We stumble and fall, and cry out to him
In our misery.
Then he hears us,
He lifts us out of darkness
And frees us from our chains.
God turns deserts into pools of water;
He brings water to the thirsty earth.
He gives the poor and the hungry a home,
They plant vines and sow seeds,
And the harvest they gather is good."

A rare and rich friendship had held David and Jonathan together since boyhood. Rare, because it had withstood the king's hatred of David, and rich because it had led each man to give the best of himself to the other.

David owed Jonathan his life. There had been times when Saul would have killed David in jealousy if Jonathan had not

But Saul would not listen. He continued to plot ways of killing David, as if he were a wild and dangerous animal. So Jonathan decided to warn his friend.

He knew where David was hiding, so he went out, as if he were hunting, with one servant, a young boy. He had arranged a signal with David, which was that he would fire three arrows and ask the boy to pick them up. David, hiding in the bushes nearby, would know by what he said whether there was good news or bad. When Jonathan had sent the boy back to the palace again with the arrows, David came out from his hiding place and the two friends embraced.

"You must leave the country," Jonathan told David. "It is new moon and my father means to hold a banquet. He has invited you to it, but I know he means to kill you if you come."

Both men wept with grief at the parting, for they feared they would never see each other again.

David had to leave the land of Israel. Where could he go to be safe from Saul's anger? The safest place of all was among the Philistines, the Israelites' traditional enemies.

So David and his men went to serve the Philistine king, Achish. They fought bravely for Achish against all the other tribes, and the king came to trust David as if he were one of his own men. But David was always sad because he was far from his own country and his great friend Jonathan.

David and Abigail

IT was the time of the sheep-shearing festival. At Carmel 3,000 sheep and 1,000 goats were being sheared for their wealthy owner, Nabal. A feast had been prepared to celebrate, and Nabal's beautiful wife Abigail was seeing to the preparations herself.

The times were good for Nabal and hard for David and his men who were camping in the wilderness nearby. David had in the past protected Nabal and the people of Carmel against the raids of the Philistines. Now he decided to ask Nabal for something in return. So he sent a messenger to remind Nabal of his past services, and ask for food and drink for himself and his men.

Nabal, who was known for his bad temper, said, "Who is this David, son of Jesse? These days every runaway slave expects to be treated like a chief!"

When David heard these words he set out in great anger to find Nabal himself and teach him a lesson. On the way he met Abigail, with several donkeys laden with gifts. She threw herself at David's feet.

"Forgive us, lord," she said, "for my husband's rude words. I have come to bring you these offerings from our house. Take them and be blessed."

David's anger left him as he looked at Abigail. He accepted her gifts and told her to go home in peace. Some days later God struck her husband down and he died.

Then David remembered the beautiful Abigail. He asked her to be his wife, and she agreed and came to him joyfully.

David the King

David the King

YET another battle between the Philistines and the Israelites was about to begin, and King Saul was afraid. God was angry with him, and the king knew it.

"Send for a witch, who can tell me what I ought to do," he said, and an old woman who was known as the Witch of Endor was brought to his tent.

"What do you want?" she asked Saul.

"I want you to cast a spell and call up the dead. Call the ghost of Samuel the prophet to speak to me," the king replied.

So she cast a spell and the ghost of Samuel appeared, wrapped in a cloak. But its message was no comfort to Saul.

"The Lord is angry with you, Saul," it said. "Tomorrow the Philistines will defeat you, and you and your son Jonathan will lie in the grave with me!"

Saul and Jonathan were both killed in the battle. David wept bitterly when he heard the news. Now he could return to Israel as its king. But he would rather have had his friend alive.

One of the first things that David did when he came to the throne was to capture the city of Jerusalem and make it Israel's new capital. It lay near the important roads which passed from Syria to Egypt and from the Mediterranean Sea to the lands further east. He built strong walls around the city and ordered carpenters and stonemasons to build him a palace inside the walls. He called Jerusalem the City of David.

Then David decided to bring the Ark of the Covenant, the scrolls and tablets on which Moses had written down the laws of God, to Jerusalem. He sent his finest soldiers to take the Ark from the small village where it had been kept ever since the Philistines sent it back. As the soldiers carried the Ark back to Jerusalem, people accompanied it all the way, dancing and singing with joy, and playing their lutes and tambourines. David ordered a great feast to be held, and danced and sang in front of the Ark along with his subjects.

Until then the Ark had been kept hidden behind curtains in the tabernacle the Israelites had carried with them through the desert. "The time has come," David said to Nathan, the prophet who was his adviser, "for me to build a great temple to the glory of God, in which the Ark will be kept."

That night God appeared to Nathan in a dream. "The time has not yet come for a temple to be built in my name," he said. "I will always love David, but one of his sons, and not he, will build my temple in Jerusalem."

David did not forget his dead friend, Jonathan. He asked if any member of Saul's family was left alive.

"Jonathan's son is still alive," his servants told him. "He is a cripple, lame in both feet."

"Where is he? Bring him to me!" cried the king. So the boy was called and when he came he kneeled down as best he could in front of the king.

David made him stand and embraced him. "I sent for you because you are the son of my great friend, Jonathan. For his sake I give back all Saul's lands to you, and for your children. Come and sit at my table—you shall be treated like one of my own sons here."

So Jonathan's son was made welcome in David's house and given a place at his table.

David and Bathsheba

David and Bathsheba

THE Ammonites were at war with Israel once again, but by now the Israelite soldiers fought so well that no warriors in the world were a match for them. David had become so confident of his men, in fact, that he no longer led them into battle personally, but sent his commanders instead while he himself remained in Jerusalem to rule the people.

It was evening. Reports of a great victory had reached David in his palace. Joab, the chief commander of his army, had defeated the Ammonites at Rabbah.

It was hot in the city, and David went up onto the flat roof of his palace, where the air was cooler and scented with jasmine and herbs from the gardens below.

As he looked down over the gardens, he saw a woman bathing in a pool nearby. She rose out of the water and her beauty seemed to fill the evening.

David watched her move away. Then he asked his servant who she was.

"She is called Bathsheba," the servant replied. "She is the wife of Uriah, one of your officers. Her husband is away fighting in Joab's army."

Night fell and darkness lay over the rooftops of Jerusalem.

"Send her to me," said David. So Bathsheba came to the king, and he fell in love with her and slept with her.

The weeks passed, and Bathsheba told David she was expecting his child. But she was still Uriah's wife. David wanted the husband to think the child was his, so he summoned the officer back to Jerusalem at once.

After he had heard his news of the war,

David gave Uriah food and drink, and sent him to his wife's room to sleep. But Uriah, who had sworn not to touch his wife until after the battle was won, would not go to her. Instead he wrapped himself in a blanket and slept in the open like his comrades in the field.

Then David wrote a letter to Joab and sent Uriah back with it. "I want Uriah to die," he wrote. "Make him fight where it is most dangerous, so that our enemies may kill him." And that is what happened.

Bathsheba wept for her husband but when the time of mourning for his death was over David took her into his palace and made her his wife.

God was angry with David because he had sinned and broken two of his commandments. He had slept with another man's wife, and he had committed murder. So God sent Nathan the prophet to the king with these words:

"There were once two men in the same city, one rich and the other poor. The rich man owned many sheep, but the poor man had only one. The lamb was life itself to him. One day a traveller came to the rich man's house and asked for food. His host kept his own sheep and stole the poor man's lamb from it. He killed it and offered it to the stranger for food."

"That man will surely be punished by God!" exclaimed the king.

"Yes, you are the man," Nathan replied.

At that moment, a servant came into the room. "Bathsheba has borne you a son," he said. "But he is dead."

Then David bowed low in grief. God's punishment had come to him.

David and Absalom

IN all Israel there was no man more handsome than Absalom, the king's eldest son. His hair was thick and heavy, and when it was cut once in a year it weighed 200 shekels on the king's scales. David loved Absalom, and gave his son chariots and horses and warriors to serve him. But Absalom wanted more; he wanted his father's throne.

Every morning he would get up early and wait at the city gate. There he would stop any man who came to ask the king for a favour and question him about it. "You are certainly in the right," he would say, "but the king will not listen to you. If I were judge I would see that justice was done to everyone." The people used to come and fall down on their knees to him. But he always raised them up and embraced them, and they loved

him all the more. They began to wish Absalom were king instead of David.

He created a network of spies and supporters, and encamped with his men in Hebron. He sent messengers to all the tribes of Israel, telling them to rise up and make him their king.

David did not want to fight his son for the throne; he preferred to give it to him. He left Jerusalem and went into exile. But it was not as simple as that. Not everyone wanted a new king, and thousands of men went along with David. The priests came, too, carrying the Ark of God with them as a sign that David was still their spiritual leader. "Take the Ark back to Jerusalem," David said to them. "If it is God's will I too will return there one day." He climbed the hills outside the city, bare-headed and bare-footed, weeping bitterly because the son whom he loved so dearly had turned away from him.

[142]

Absalom would not rest until he had the whole country under him. He declared war on his father. So David mustered his army together on the banks of the Jordan. He put Joab in command, telling him: "Whatever happens, deal gently with my son."

The two armies met in the forest of Ephron, and the battle between them lasted all day. By nightfall, most of Absalom's men lay dead and Absalom himself had fled.

As he galloped through the woods on his mule, with David's men close behind, Absalom's long hair caught in the boughs of a tree. He was swept out of his saddle and hung there, dangling, until his enemies came up. They sent for Joab, who killed him.

When David heard of Absalom's death he climbed into a tower above the city gate and cried:

"Oh, Absalom, my son, I wish I had died instead of you! Oh, Absalom, my son!"

The Death of David

David was an old man and he wanted one of his sons to succeed him. "A king," he said to them, "must be just; he must see that the commandments of God are obeyed. If he is an inspiration to his people, he will be as dear to them as the light of the morning when the sun rises, and as the fresh grass that springs out of the earth when the sun shines on it after the rain." Then he chose Solomon, the son of Bathsheba, to be king in his place.

David grew weaker, and although they wrapped blankets around him, he could not keep warm. He knew that death was not far away.

"I am going the way of all things on earth," he said to Solomon his son, who was standing by his bed. "You must be strong, and show the people that you are a man. You must lead the people of Israel to do what is right in the eyes of God. As long as they obey God and follow his commandments he will protect them. He will ensure that the house of David shall never fall, that there shall always be a king of Israel."

Then David slept, and in his sleep he died. He was buried beside his forefathers in Jerusalem, the city he had made Israel's capital and called the City of David.

Solomon Becomes King

KING DAVID's son Solomon was not first in the line to the throne, although his father had chosen him as his successor. But his mother was David's favourite wife, Bathsheba, and she wanted her only son to be king. This is how it happened.

David's eldest son Adonijah, a handsome and headstrong man, expected to inherit the throne. One day, tired of waiting any longer for his father to die, he declared himself king. People were shocked, among them Nathan the prophet, who came to Bathsheba and told her.

"If you want your son to be king," he said, "you had better go to your husband quickly and tell him what is happening."

She went to see David, who was very near his death. "Once you swore to me that our son Solomon would be king after you," she said to her husband. "Now I hear that Adonijah has set himself up as your successor. People don't like it; there is talk of civil war. All Israel is waiting for you to declare the truth."

With almost his last breath the old king said, "Let Solomon ride my horse and wear my crown. Call Zadok the priest. Together they must go to Gihon, where Zadok must take the holy oil from God's tabernacle and anoint Solomon as king."

David's orders were obeyed. A great crowd of people led Solomon from Jerusalem to Gihon, headed by Zadok the priest and Nathan the prophet. Zadok took the flask of oil and anointed Solomon. The trumpets rang out and the people deserted from Adonijah's camp and came running to Gihon to join the procession escorting the new king back to Jerusalem. Pipes played, and from everywhere the shout went up:

"Long live King Solomon!"

The Judgment of Solomon

SOLOMON was still a young man when he became king. Unlike his father, who had been brought up as a shepherd boy, Solomon had lived at court all his life. He knew the difficulties that faced anyone who tried to be the Israelites' leader, and he knew that he could not do it without the help of God.

One night God came to him in a dream.

"What do you want from me, Solomon?" he asked the young king.

"I want to be great, like my father," Solomon replied. "He was an old and wise man when he died. I am young and inexperienced. Give me wisdom, God, the wisdom that old men have, and a knowledge of good and evil. Give me the skill to listen to others now, while I am young, and throughout my life, so that I may learn from them. Give me eyes that see clearly, and what I see, let me understand. Give me goodness and honesty, so that I may serve you as my father did."

God was pleased. He said to Solomon:

"Because you did not ask for riches, nor for a long life, nor for the blood of your enemies, but for these other things, you shall receive them all, and much more besides. For as long as men live, they will praise the wisdom and the justice of Solomon."

Solomon did not have to wait long to put his new gifts to use. On his return to Jerusalem he found two women waiting at the palace for him. They had come to hear the highest judge in all Israel, the king himself, pass judgment on them.

Solomon seated himself on the throne and the women were brought before him. Each carried in her arms a baby wrapped in a cloth. One was kicking and crying; the other lay quite still. It was dead. The dead and the living children were laid at the king's feet.

"My lord," one of the women began, "I am the mother of the living child—"

"It's mine," the other woman cut in. "It was born to me on the same night that this woman had her baby. She lay on her child, and it died."

"No, my lord, that woman is lying. It was she who slept after her child was born, and she who smothered it by lying on it, so that it died. My child is alive. It is here, in front of you. Say that it is mine!" she begged.

King Solomon looked first at one woman and then at the other. Then he looked down at the baby kicking at his feet.

"Which of you is telling the truth?" he asked.

"I am, my lord," one of them said.

"While I slept this woman came and stole my child and put her dead one in its place."

"You are lying!" the other woman exclaimed.

The baby began to cry. Solomon looked down at it again, and then back to the women.

"One child cannot belong to two mothers," he said. "One of you is lying to me. Which one is it?"

"Not I, my lord," insisted one woman.

"Not I," cried the other.

King Solomon turned to one of the guards standing behind his throne.

"Bring me a sword," he commanded.

The soldier brought a sword and the king ordered him to take it out of its sheath and come closer to the living baby. Then he

himself turned to the people who were gathered in the court and addressed them.

"God has called these two women before us," he said, "and they have brought me this child. Each wants me to tell her she is the real mother. Since both want the child, they must each have one half of it!"

With that the young king signalled to the soldier with the sword.

"This child shall be cut in two and divided equally between you," he said.

There was a terrible silence. Just as the sword was about to come down over the child the real mother ran forward. She caught the soldier by the arm, crying out:

"No! Don't kill him! Let her have my son!"

King Solomon turned to her. The soldier lowered his sword.

"Keep your son," the king said gently. He picked the baby up and put it into her arms.

[147]

The Building of the Temple

For nearly 500 years the Ark of the Covenant, containing the tablets and scrolls of the law, had been carried around by the people of Israel. Ever since Moses had put the tablets into the Ark, it had been kept in its tabernacle, and had travelled from deserts to villages, from towns to cities, until at last King David had brought it to Jerusalem, intending to build it a permanent home.

It was the fourth year of Solomon's reign, and already he was richer and more powerful than any king before him.

"The time has come for me to build a

great Temple for the Lord's Ark," he said. "It will be made from the finest materials and by the most skilful craftsmen in the world."

Solomon supervised every detail. He sent to every part of Israel for the best materials, and if he was not satisfied with what his men brought back he sent them to other countries to find something better.

The king of Tyre sent cypresses from his forests to the north of Israel; great rafts of wood were shipped down the coast and carried inland from the ports by caravans of camels. The giant cedars from Mount Leba-

non were felled and brought to Jerusalem.

The metals were mined and smelted in the desert far to the southeast of Jerusalem. They were cast in moulds made of clay and then taken north for the craftsmen to finish. The work on them was supervised by a man named Hiram, the most skilled worker in bronze that the world had yet known.

The stone was hewn and chiselled at the quarries, so that no sound of hammer or axe or tool of any kind should be heard in the Temple grounds.

Sweet-smelling cedar wood was used for the walls and ceilings, and fir trees were sawn up for the floors. Wood from wild olive trees was used to carve two cherubims, each fifteen feet high, to guard the Holy of Holies where the Ark of the Covenant itself was to be kept.

Thousands of men were set to work quarrying the stone and shaping it into square blocks for the outer buildings. Thousands more carved and moulded the interior of the Temple. Metal workers were brought in from other lands to hammer and work the gold and silver which covered the altars. The rooms were hung with tapestries woven with gold and silk thread dyed in rich and rare colours.

In the end King Solomon's Temple became more like a walled city than a single building.

The Temple took seven years to build. When the work was finished Solomon brought all King David's treasures and added them to his own. He brought ancient lamps and tongs, spoons and bowls, all made of gold, and dedicated them at the altar of God.

Then he called together the high priests and the soldiers, and the heads of the twelve tribes to join in a great procession and bring the Ark of God into the Temple he had built for it, to show the glory of God.

The Visit of the Queen of Sheba

As God had foretold, Solomon's fame spread throughout the world. People came to hear his words of wisdom, and stayed to admire his palaces. He had created a world of unbelievable splendour around him. Gardens with fountains playing in them, stables filled with swift horses, chariots made of gold, a Temple that was like a great, bright jewel—all these dazzled the whole world with their magnificence.

Merchants came to Solomon's court with their pack animals laden with rare and precious goods from distant countries, and took news of its splendour back with them. His own camel trains crossed deserts and his great ships ploughed across the seas, further than ever before. News of this kingdom reached Sheba, where a wise queen ruled. She decided to see Solomon and his country for herself.

Because she was a queen, and as proud and mighty as any monarch on earth, she brought with her splendid presents for the king. Her camels and her slaves carried herbs

to heal and spices to eat, oils to anoint the body and perfume to sweeten it. She brought gifts of gold and silks and precious stones.

The arrival of the queen of Sheba was as splendid as anything that King Solomon's city had ever seen. Solomon, dressed in magnificent robes heavy with gold, awaited her, sitting on his throne. The queen came in, clothed in silks and pearls, rubies and damask, with a retinue of slaves carrying her gifts. She stood in front of him.

Then the queen tested Solomon's wisdom. As was customary in those days, she set him riddles. She questioned him about everything under the sun, and on every point the king answered her. His words were as bright and clear as his own jewels.

Then the king led her to a banquet in his palace. The food he served was cooked with spices and herbs as rare as those the queen of Sheba had brought him, and rich perfumes scented the air. When they had eaten together the queen said to Solomon:

"All the things that people say about you are true, though I did not believe them until I came and saw you with my own eyes. But the stories do not tell even half of what is here; your wisdom and your splendour are greater than any praise that has been given them. Let me stay a while longer, my lord, to see all the riches that your God has given you."

Then Solomon showed her everything in the land: the ministries that governed the people, the temples and their priests, the courts of justice. He showed her the great ships at anchor, the mines and the furnaces where the smiths smelted metal. He showed her, above all, the place where thinkers from all nations came together to talk and listen —to listen to Solomon as he spoke with the wisdom and understanding that God had given him.

Then the queen blessed the God of Solomon and the land of Israel, and went home.

[151]

Solomon had grown great through his wisdom; he remained great through his power over people. In time, however, this power became dangerous and the king was corrupted by it. He introduced a form of slavery which the Israelites hated. He took more and more of the country's wealth for himself, to pay for his ships and his chariots, his palaces and his wives. Above all, he began to worship other gods.

Solomon's wives were the daughters of neighbouring kings. Thus he remained at peace with the countries around him, and also acquired great wealth from their trade with Israel. He allowed each of his wives to worship the gods of her own religion, and had temples built for them. In time Solomon himself grew interested in these gods, then he began to worship them. He offered sacrifices to them, within sight of God's holy Temple.

In anger, God told Solomon, "You have broken my commandments, and have brought suffering on Israel. For the sake of your father David, the country will remain one kingdom until you die. Then it will divide into two nations and they will be at war with each other. The ten tribes of the north will fight the two tribes of the south, and their days will be full of evil doings."

The Ravens Feed Elijah

THE time of greatness for Israel was over. As God had foretold, its people were divided into two kingdoms, that of Israel in the north, and that of Judah in the south. The people in both kingdoms stopped worshipping God, and did many evil things. Their kings were evil too—but the worst of them all was Ahab, king of Israel.

Ahab had made himself king over the ten tribes of the north, and had taken as his wife Jezebel, daughter of the king of Tyre. Together they worshipped Baal, and built idols and temples to him. Queen Jezebel ordered that the prophets of the true God be put to death, and only one of them, Elijah, managed to escape and hide in the hills of Gilead.

One day Elijah appeared before King Ahab. He spoke abruptly:

"I am the prophet of the true God, the God of Israel. Because of the evil in you and in your people there will be no more rain until God wishes it."

He left the king's palace as swiftly as he had come, before any of the guards could arrest him.

God warned him, "Go east, Elijah, and hide from the king's anger. Go to the brook of Kerith where the water is pure. Drink it; I will provide the food."

So Elijah hid in the desert hills, sleeping under bushes and in caves. At sunrise and sunset every day God sent him food: the great black ravens of Kerith brought fresh meat and bread for the prophet.

The Priests of Baal

THERE was a great drought in Ahab's kingdom. Elijah had told the king there would be no rain until God spoke to him again, and for nearly three years God was silent. Elijah left Israel and went to live with a poor widow and her son in the kingdom of Tyre. Then one day God spoke to him and told him it was time to go back to King Ahab.

By this time there was a famine in Israel because of the drought. Ahab sent for his chamberlain Obadiah. "This drought is burning up my land," he said to him, "and the people are dying. Go out and search for hidden springs of water, so that we can keep ourselves and our animals alive."

Obadiah set off to look for water, and on his way he met Elijah. "Go and tell your master that I have returned," the prophet said.

When Ahab and Elijah met face to face the king accused him of bringing drought and famine to Israel.

"Not I, my lord, have done this," said Elijah. "But you in your wickedness—you and your false god Baal. The rains will come back. But first you and all your priests and people must meet me on Mount Carmel."

Ahab had little choice. He ordered the priests of Baal to assemble, and thousands of people came to Mount Carmel to see them. Elijah stepped forward:

"How much longer are you going to sit on the fence?" he asked the crowds. "Either Baal is the true god, or God is."

The people said nothing. Elijah went on:

"I say that God is. Here are 450 priests who say that Baal is. So let us both prepare a bull for sacrifice. Let us cut it up and lay it on wood, and call on our gods to set fire to it. The god who answers by fire is the true God."

The people shouted their agreement, and the bulls were killed. The priests of Baal prayed and danced wildly around the altar, shouting, "Baal, Baal, answer us." But there was no answer.

Elijah mocked them. "Call louder," he

said, "maybe Baal cannot hear you." So the priests cried louder, and cut their bodies with knives so that the blood ran down. No answer came from Baal.

Elijah turned to the people and beckoned them to come closer. Then he built an altar to God. Three times he poured water over it, drenching the wood and the meat. Then he came forward and prayed:

"Now, God of Abraham, of Isaac and of Israel, let the people see that you alone are God."

A silence fell. Then a great roar of fire sprang up from the altar. The flames burned the bull, the wood, the great stones and even the water in the trench around the altar. Nothing remained.

The people fell on their knees. "The Lord is God!" they cried out. "The Lord is God!"

"Seize these priests," Elijah told them, pointing to the priests of Baal, "for they have brought you great evil."

When the people had killed the priests Elijah turned to Ahab.

"Go back now," he said, "and eat and drink, for I hear the sound of rain."

[155]

The Still, Small Voice

JEZEBEL the queen was angry when she heard what had happened, and swore to have Elijah put to death in revenge for her priests. Elijah did not wait. He left Jerusalem and fled into the desert. There he lay down exhausted and dispirited under a bush, and prayed for death.

Instead, he fell asleep, and while he was

sleeping an angel touched him and said:

"Come and eat."

Elijah awoke. He was hungry and thirsty and he was all alone in the desert. Yet he could smell the sweet smell of newly baked bread. He looked around him in surprise. On a stone by his elbow, lay a loaf of flat, hot bread and beside it was a pitcher of water, clear and fresh. Gratefully, the prophet ate the food God had sent him and drank the cool water.

When Elijah had finished his meal, God spoke to him. "Why are you here, Elijah?" he asked.

"Because Israel has turned against you, Lord. Jezebel has sworn to kill me, and I have fled to save my life."

"Go to Mount Horeb, the sacred mountain," God replied, "and I will be there."

Elijah travelled for 40 days and 40 nights. When he came to the sacred mountain a great wind sprang up. The prophet took refuge in a cave, listening and watching in fear as the wind tore trees out of the ground and shattered rocks. Then it died down, and after the wind there was an earthquake. The ground cracked and trembled, and a great fire leaped up from it. The flames covered the mountain, and died away.

God was not in the earthquake, in the wind, or in the fire. He was in the quiet and the darkness of the night. Calmly, gently, in a still, small voice, God spoke to Elijah, telling him about Israel's future. A young man named Jehu was to become its king, and Elijah himself would be joined by a new prophet named Elisha, who would be his pupil and who would one day take his place.

Naboth's Vineyard

CLOSE beside the palace lay a large vineyard that belonged to a man named Naboth, who lived in the city of Jezreel. King Ahab liked to look down on it and in time he began to wish it were his. He said to Naboth:

"Let me have your vineyard so that I can make it into a garden. I will give you other land in exchange, or if you prefer, you can have its price in silver."

"I want neither," said Naboth. "This vineyard was my father's, and his father's before him. We will never give it up."

The king went back to his palace in a fury. When she learned the reason, his wife Jezebel was angry too. "Are you or are you not king here?" she demanded. "Leave it to me—I will make you a present of the land."

She wrote a letter in the king's name and bribed some dishonest judges. She brought false witnesses to accuse Naboth of treason and sacrilege—of speaking evil of the king and of cursing God—and he was found guilty. He was taken out of the city of Jezreel and stoned to death. Now the vineyard belonged to the king.

Before long God's judgment came on him, swift and terrible. "Your son's blood will flow where Naboth's blood flowed," the prophet Elijah told him. "And jackals will eat the body of Jezebel."

The Parting of Elijah and Elisha

AFTER Elijah came Elisha. Elijah had met him one day, ploughing in the valley of the Jordan, and God told him that the young man was to be his successor as prophet. The older man threw his cloak over Elisha as a symbol that he was calling him to be his pupil. At once Elisha stopped ploughing, went to say goodbye to his family, and joined Elijah in his work.

The old prophet and the new had been together about seven years when Elijah said to Elisha:

"I must leave you and go on a journey."

"I will come with you," said Elisha, and they set out together for Bethel. Both prophets knew that this would be Elijah's last journey, his journey to God. So they walked towards Bethel, preaching to the people about the only true God, and teaching them to renounce all others.

When they reached the town, Elijah said:

"Stay here, Elisha. I must go on to Jericho."

Elisha knew that his teacher's time on earth was short. "I will come with you," he insisted.

At Jericho they were met by a group of other prophets.

"Do you know that God will take your master away from us today?" they asked Elisha.

"I know," Elisha replied. "Don't say any more."

The old prophet turned to Elisha. "Stay here," he said. "God is calling me. I must go to the river Jordan as he commands."

"I will come with you," Elisha replied.

So they left Jericho, and 50 of the prophets went with them. When they reached the banks of the river the prophets saw Elijah take off his cloak and roll it up. They saw him strike the river with it. The river divided and the two men crossed over the dry river bed and disappeared from the prophets' view.

As they crossed, Elijah said:

"What can I do for you before I go?"

"Give me your spirit," Elisha replied. "Give me a double portion of it, like the inheritance a father gives to his eldest son."

Elijah understood. "I shall soon be taken from you by a miracle," he said. "If you see this take place, you will know that God has given you my spirit. If not, then God has not chosen you."

Suddenly the sky opened and a chariot drawn by horses of fire came down to them. A whirlwind arose. It came between Elijah and Elisha and lifted Elijah into the chariot, and the chariot into the sky.

"My father, my father!" Elisha cried. "The horses and the chariots of Israel!"

He picked up the cloak that Elijah had dropped, and put it over his shoulders. The spirit of Elijah was in him.

He went back to the Jordan and struck the river water with Elijah's cloak. The water divided before him, and he walked over the dry bed to join the prophets who were waiting for him on the other side.

Elisha Cures Naaman

IN the nearby kingdom of Syria there lived a great soldier called Naaman. As commander of the army he had won many battles and the king valued him. Then he fell ill with leprosy, and his skin was covered with white sores that would not heal.

A little slave girl came to Naaman's wife and said:

"I know a man who can cure him."

The girl was from Israel, and had been kidnapped from her home by the Syrian soldiers on one of their raids across the border.

"There is a prophet who lives in Samaria; he will cure my lord," she added.

When the Syrian king heard about the prophet he was filled with hope for Naaman.

"Go at once to Israel," he said, "and take these gifts with you. I myself will write a letter to the king, asking him to cure you of your leprosy." He gave Naaman gold and silver and fine clothes for the journey.

When the king of Israel read the letter he was filled with dismay. "Am I a god?" he exclaimed. "How can I cure this man? It must be a plot. The king of Syria wants to pick a quarrel with me!"

But Elisha, who had also heard about Naaman's visit, sent a messenger to invite the Syrian general to his house.

"If the man comes to me," he said, "he will know that there is a prophet in Israel."

So Naaman came with his horses and chariots and stood outside Elisha's house. He waited for the prophet to appear. But Elisha's power was so great that he could cure Naaman without seeing him. He sent a messenger out to say:

"Go and wash in the river Jordan seven times and your skin will be healed."

Naaman lost his temper. "I didn't come all this way to be told to wash myself," he stormed. "The least your prophet could do is to come out and speak to me himself. He

should call on his God, wave his hand over me, offer sacrifices. If I had wanted to wash in a river I would have stayed in Damascus; our rivers there are cleaner than yours!" And he went away in a rage.

"Come now," his servant argued with him. "If Elisha had asked you to do something difficult, you would have done it without question. Why don't you do something that is simple?"

So Naaman turned back to the Jordan. He dipped himself in the river seven times.

Each time the leprosy grew less, until at last his skin was as clear as a child's.

He came back to Elisha. "Now I know that your God is the true God," he said. "Will you accept these gifts from me as a token of my gratitude?"

But Elisha would take nothing. "It was not I who saved you but my God," he said.

"Then, since you want nothing for healing me," Naaman replied, "let me make your God my God. From now on I will stop praying to my old gods and worship your God."

The Anointing of Jehu

GOD had told the prophet Elijah that a young soldier named Jehu was destined to be the next king of Israel. But Elijah died, and it was left to Elisha to anoint him.

Elisha called one of his followers, a young prophet, and said:

"Go to Ramoth-Gilead where Jehu is stationed. You will find him among the other officers. Tell him to come with you to a quiet place. Anoint him as king of Israel, and then make your escape."

The prophet went to Ramoth-Gilead, and found Jehu there with his fellow officers. "Come with me," he said to the young soldier. "I have a message for you."

Jehu went with him into an inner room. There the prophet unclasped the flask of holy oil he carried on his belt and poured it over Jehu.

"In the name of God I anoint you as king over Israel," he said. Then he disappeared.

Jehu returned to the other soldiers.

"Well," his friends asked, "what did that man want with you? He seemed to be in a trance, like a madman or a prophet."

"He was a prophet, and he has anointed me as king of Israel," Jehu replied. "It is God's will that I destroy the family of Ahab because of the evil he has brought to our country."

Then the soldiers blew their trumpets. They pulled off their cloaks and spread them on the ground for Jehu to walk on. "Jehu is our king!" they shouted.

King Ahab had died and his son Jehoram was now king of Israel. Jehoram had been wounded while fighting against the Syrians, and he took refuge in the city of Jezreel to recover his strength. The king of Judah came to visit him there.

Hearing that Jehoram was sick, Jehu gathered his men together and advanced on Jezreel in his chariot. A watchman in Jezreel saw Jehu's chariot in the distance approaching the city, and sent a warning to the two kings. Jehoram grew afraid. "Send a horseman to meet him and ask, 'Do you come in peace?'" he ordered his men.

When the horseman did not return Jehoram sent out a second messenger with the same question. He too did not return, for Jehu had forced them both to stay with him and join his soldiers.

Then the two kings grew even more afraid. They ordered their chariots to be harnessed with horses, and fled as fast as they could. Just as they were passing Naboth's vineyard Jehu caught up with the king of Israel. With an arrow from his bow he shot Jehoram and killed him. Jehu's men threw the body over the wall into the vineyard. The first part of God's curse on Ahab was fulfilled.

Jehu returned to Jezreel, driving his chariot hard all the way. Queen Jezebel had heard of the killing of her son and knew that her own death could not be far away. The proud daughter of the king of Tyre prepared to meet her end defiantly. She dressed herself and made herself up as if for a state

occasion. Then she waited for her enemy to arrive.

As Jehu drove his chariot through the city gate she called down to him from the wall above:

"Murderer! Do you bring peace?"

Jehu looked up at the mocking queen.

"Throw her down!" he commanded her servants.

They did, and the horses trampled her body underfoot. It was left lying in the waste ground under the city wall, and there the jackals tore it to pieces, just as Elijah had prophesied so many years before.

[163]

The Reign of Joash

IN the southern kingdom of Judah, Athaliah, the daughter of Jezebel, wanted to be queen. She had every possible rival killed, including her own grandsons. Her daughter managed to save the smallest boy, Joash, and hid him in the Temple, where he was brought up by the high priest Jehoiada.

For six years Athaliah ruled as queen of Judah. Then Jehoiada called all the royal guards and the priests to the Temple and led them before Joash, the late king's son. He handed each captain a shield and spear, and reminded the soldiers that the weapons had been King David's and that the boy was of David's family. Then Jehoiada placed

the crown on his head and everyone shouted: "Long live the king!"

Athaliah heard the shouting and hurried to the Temple. "Treason!" she called out, as she saw the new king standing by a pillar. But Jehoiada ordered two guards to take her outside the Temple and kill her.

Once he was king Joash had all Athaliah's temples to Baal destroyed. He ordered the great Temple to be repaired and had a chest placed beside the altar, so that people could leave money offerings to God inside it.

But in time he too did wrong and God punished him. The Syrians invaded Judah and Joash was killed by his own servants.

The Death of Elisha

ELISHA the prophet lived to a great old age. His single aim in life had been to bring back the ancient worship of God to the Israelites, and to throw out the heathen gods that they had set up and worshipped in God's place. He trained younger men to carry the message to the people, and founded centres throughout the land where priests and prophets taught.

One day, while he was visiting such a centre, he watched the young men at work. One of them said to him:

"We have to go down to the Jordan to cut more wood. Will you come with us?"

"I will," Elisha replied.

When they reached the river they began cutting down the trees. Suddenly one of their axes broke and its head flew off into the water.

"Oh, master!" the woodcutter exclaimed in distress, "that axe doesn't belong to me!" Then Elisha performed a miracle. He cut off another piece of wood and threw it where the axe had sunk. The metal rose to the surface and floated towards the shore. The woodcutter reached out for it with awe, and fastened it back on its shaft.

Another time the enemies of Israel had

have no spies here—but Elisha the prophet can hear every word you speak in your bed-chamber."

"Then we must kill him," said the king. "Go and find out where he is, so that I can take him prisoner."

When the king's spies returned, they reported that Elisha was in a city called Dothan.

"Take my horses and chariots," the king commanded his generals, "and an army of 1,000 men. Blockade the city, capture Elisha and bring him to me."

The people living in Dothan were filled with panic when such a great army appeared and camped in the hills around them.

"Oh Lord," Elisha prayed to God, "open their eyes so that they can see."

Suddenly a bright light shone on the hills and all the people began to cry out in wonder. "Look!" they cried. "The hills are on fire! There are horses and chariots of fire all around the city! God has sent them to protect us!"

In time the prophet grew old and weak; his death was not far off. As he lay dying the king of Israel came to visit him. He was sad, but Elisha reminded him of his duty as leader of the chosen people.

"Take your bow and arrows," he said, "and open the window that faces east."

The king did so, and Elisha laid his hands on the younger man's, to guide them. He shot an arrow through the air, and then another one.

"You will win a victory for God, and a victory over your enemy," Elisha said. "Now strike the ground with the remaining arrows."

The king struck three times, and then he paused.

"Oh, you have stopped too soon!" cried the prophet. "Now God will give you three victories over Syria, and no more!"

Then Elisha closed his eyes and died.

blockaded the city where Elisha was. For many weeks the Syrian army had been raiding deep into the surrounding country, but each time they had found that the people there, forewarned, had driven off their flocks and herds, and had hidden their stores. The king of Syria began to suspect that there were spies in his camp.

"No, my lord," said his soldiers. "We

Josiah and Isaiah's Prophecies

TIME passed, and one king followed another on the throne of Judah. Yet again they allowed the people to worship foreign gods, and yet again God was angry.

Then came a king named Josiah. He was determined to bring the Israelites back to worshipping God once more. When he was sixteen he began clearing away all the altars and temples to foreign gods in the land. He left only one temple, the Temple of God in Jerusalem, for the people to use for worship. One Temple, one God, was Josiah's command, and the people obeyed.

One day, as the priests were clearing out the dark corners of the building, they came across a book. It was the forgotten Book of the Law, which a prophet named Isaiah had collected together in an earlier time, when the country had been beset by enemies within and without. At that time the Assyrians had been threatening to destroy Judah, and her own king was desecrating the Temple of God with idol worship. Isaiah had compiled the Book of the Law as a message for future generations to take to heart.

Now it was placed before Josiah. The king read Isaiah's prophecies and understood the full meaning of God's words. Because the Israelites had broken God's commandments to Moses, not once but many times, they were to lose everything they had. Their king was to die and their country was to be destroyed.

The prophecies also foretold the coming of a new leader, who would bring peace to the sorely troubled Israelites, a man who would be a saviour, a redeemer, a deliverer of his people. But before that there would be a time of terrible hardship and suffering—and there was no way of avoiding it.

The Fall and Destruction of Jerusalem

THE northern kingdom of Israel was destroyed and Samaria, its capital, laid waste. Its people had put up a brave fight, but finally the armies of the king of Assyria had swept down on the ten tribes and wiped them out. Those who survived were mostly carried off as slaves and prisoners. Other people were brought into the country—refugees and captives from other conquered lands, who set up their own idols and worshipped them.

The people in the south, in the land of Judah, saw what had happened to their fellow Israelites and were terrified. The Assyrians were powerful warriors and their conquest of Israel would not satisfy them for long. The people of Judah feared that their own kingdom and their beloved Temple would soon go the same way. They came to an uneasy agreement with the Assyrians, and handed over much of their wealth in exchange for peace.

A generation went by, and the people of Judah were surrounded by new enemies. The Medes, the Babylonians, the Egyptians and the Assyrians were all fighting for land and power. In time the Assyrians were conquered in their turn, and their great capital of Nineveh was destroyed. The Medes and the Babylonians were the new victors, and the kingdom of Judah now came under the power of Babylon.

[168]

A king named Nebuchadnezzar came to the throne in Babylon. He imposed heavy taxes on the people of the neighbouring countries. The Israelites left in Judah were too few to be able to fight the Babylonians and have any hope of defeating them. Jeremiah, the prophet who led the country at that time, urged his people to keep the peace.

But the king of Judah, Josiah's son, was an impatient man. Against all odds he rallied his people together and marched against the enemy. His father had done the same, and had been killed in battle against the Assyrians. Now it was the son's turn, and

he too was killed—fighting the Babylonians.

Nebuchadnezzar was ruthless. He captured Judah's leaders and sent them to Babylon. Then he took the soldiers and the skilled workers and made them his slaves. He sent all the best men from Judah to his country. Then he chose a new king for Judah: Zedekiah, Josiah's second son.

The prophet Jeremiah stayed on in Jerusalem. He warned the new king, "Don't oppose your enemy. If you obey him, God will be with you."

For nine years the king listened to Jeremiah. Then he could stand it no longer. He rebelled against the enemy and threw out every Babylonian who was living in the city. He closed the city gates and barred each entrance. Then he waited for the Babylonian army to attack in revenge.

It was a long siege. The people of Jerusalem withstood both hunger and heat, but at last death from both began to spread through the city. King Zedekiah slipped out to try to get help from across the Jordan.

He was captured, and killed. The Babylonians entered Jerusalem and smashed and burned everything in it. The great Temple of Solomon was pulled down and destroyed. The history of Israel, it seemed, was at an end as the prisoners marched into exile.

The Jewish Prisoners in Babylon

"By the rivers of Babylon we sat down, and we wept when we remembered Israel," sang the people in exile, who now became known as Jews, because they came from the land of Judah.

No place could have been more different from the rocky hills of Judah than the open plains of Babylonia where King Nebuchadnezzar brought them. The great rivers Euphrates and Tigris were the boundaries of Babylonia, and the Jewish prisoners would sit in the shade of the trees that lined the river and sing sadly about their life:

"There, on the willow trees, we hung our
  harps.
How can we dance or play our lutes
When sorrow fills our hearts?
How can we sing the Lord's song
In a foreign land?"

But Jeremiah the prophet sent a message of hope.

"God has not forgotten you," the old man wrote to the exiles from Jerusalem. "Keep his commandments and pray for his help. Build houses, work, have children. Make gardens in Babylon, grow your food there, and eat it. Trust in God, for in time he will bring you back to Israel again. He will gather all the exiles together from every nation, from every corner of the earth where he scattered them in his anger. Call to God, and

he will listen to you. Look for him, and he will appear. He will give back everything that has been lost, and will make his chosen people great again."

The Jews were filled with hope once more. They built altars to God and worshipped him. They elected priests and elders to represent them. They worked hard for Nebuchadnezzar, as engineers on his canals, as smiths on Babylon's great bronze gates, and as masons on the hanging gardens whose beauty had already made them famous as one of the wonders of the world. As their families grew larger, the Jews grew steadily more powerful, and God was pleased with them.

Time passed. Another prophet appeared, younger and more forceful than Jeremiah. His name was Ezekiel. He came to Babylon from Jerusalem, and he taught the Jews

that their God was with them, even in their exile, and that they were to prepare for their return to their native land.

"God came to me in a dream," he told them, "and in the dream you appeared as dry bones, lying in a field. Listen to what the Lord said to me. He said, 'I will breathe on these dry bones, and they will live. I will grow muscles around them, and flesh will cover them, and skin will cover the flesh. When I breathe on them they will rise again as my people.'

"Then I heard a sound of shaking," he went on. "Each bone linked itself to another bone. As I looked on, muscles grew on the bones, and flesh. Then I prayed for a wind to come and breathe on them, and it did. The spirit of God breathed on them in the wind, and they became a great army of people. They became the people of Israel."

The King's Dream

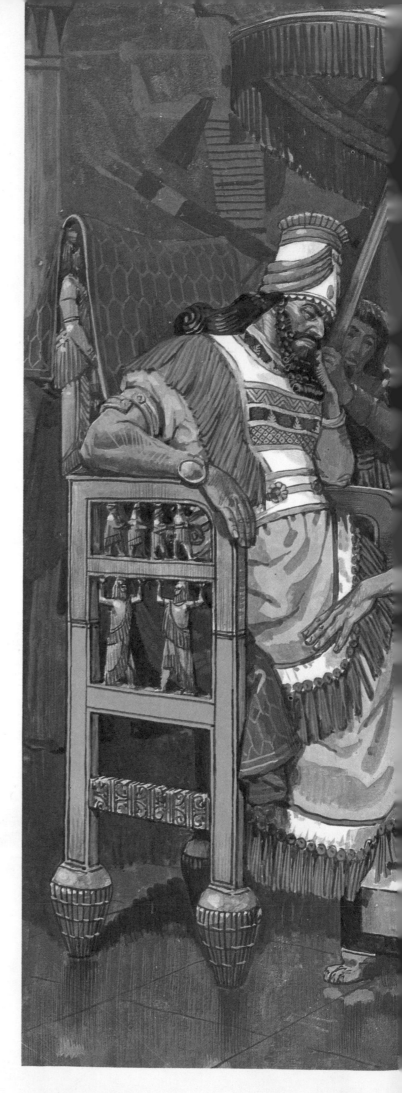

King NEBUCHADNEZZAR was troubled because he kept having fearful dreams. He summoned the wise men of Babylon and asked them to interpret them.

"Describe your dream, my lord, and we will tell you its meaning," the magicians said.

The king replied angrily, "I did not call you here to ask me questions, but to answer mine. If you cannot tell me what my dream was—and then what it means—I shall have you all executed as impostors!"

The magicians hedged. "No one can describe another man's dream," they pleaded.

"Very well," the king replied. "You have no right to call yourselves magicians. You have lied, and every one of you must die!"

A young man named Daniel was among those sentenced to death. He was a Jew, captured and taken from Judah by the Babylonians. He asked to be brought to the king, and God helped him to interpret what Nebuchadnezzar had dreamed.

"In your dream you saw a giant," he told the king. "It was made of gold and silver, bronze and iron and clay. While you looked, a stone struck the giant and he crumbled away. The stone grew into a great mountain that covered the earth. The giant's limbs, my lord, are the heathen kingdoms of the world. The stone that destroys them is the kingdom of God, which will grow big enough to cover the whole earth. Not I, my lord, but my God has told you your dream."

Nebuchadnezzar bowed. "The God of gods has spoken," he said.

The Golden Statue

KING NEBUCHADNEZZAR's capital of Babylon was more magnificent than any other city on earth. He had conquered other countries and had carried the most gifted of their peoples back as his captives to work for Babylon. He had ordered a great wall to be built around the city, pierced by 100 gates of bronze. Houses several storeys high had been built and painted in dazzling colours, to line the wide avenues of Babylon. He had drawn up the plans for the great network of canals that surrounded the city and made the earth fertile.

Nebudchadnezzar wanted the fame of Babylon to reach still greater heights. He made a statue that surpassed all others in magnificence, and had it cast in gold. It was so big that there was no room for it inside the city. It had to be erected on the plains outside. When the colossus was finished, it was 90 feet high and nine feet across, and it towered over the country around.

King Nebuchadnezzar ordered all his officials and all the people under them to attend the dedication of the idol. Music was written for the occasion, and a great feast was prepared.

When the day came the people from all around gathered in obedience to the king's commands. The king's musicians sounded a fanfare on their trumpets and everyone fell silent, waiting for the herald to tell them what was going to happen.

"People of all lands and every language,"

he announced. "You have assembled here today at the king's command. He wishes you to worship this golden statue. This will be the signal: when the music of the king's horns and trumpets and harps fills the air, and the singers break into song, you must all fall on your knees, bow until your foreheads touch the ground, and worship. Any man who does not worship the statue will be thrown into a furnace and burned to death."

A great stillness hung over the vast crowd of people. Then a burst of song and music seemed to shake the air and make the ground tremble.

Some of the people fell on their knees to worship the idol. They pressed their hands to their faces as if trying to blot out the sight of such a terrifying power. Others threw themselves down onto the ground, hiding their faces in the dust. Men and women threw up their arms, crying out:

"Almighty power, great god of our great King Nebuchadnezzar! You fill us with terror—do not destroy us completely! Have mercy on us for we are your slaves!"

They beat on the ground and the dust rose in clouds and filled the air.

King Nebuchadnezzar looked down at his subjects and was pleased. It was a glorious moment for Babylon, and the power of her king seemed to have no bounds.

Nebuchadnezzar's triumph was cut short. A messenger ran up to him, and said:

"My lord, some wise men are here and want to speak to you!"

"Let them come forward," the king replied.

The men advanced and knelt down respectfully at Nebuchadnezzar's feet.

"Long live the king!" they exclaimed. "Your majesty has issued an order that every man must fall down and worship the statue. Any man who does not is to be thrown into the furnace. There are three Jews who have disobeyed your command. They say they do not believe in your god, and they refuse to worship an idol. Their names are Shadrach, Meshach and Abednego.

"Punish them as they deserve, your majesty! Throw them into a blazing furnace!"

Shadrach, Meshach and Abed-nego

IT was not the first time that Shadrach, Meshach and Abed-nego had caught the king's eye. As children they had been hand-picked from among all the exiled Jews in Babylon to serve in the royal household. The fourth in their group was Daniel, a fine, quick-witted boy, the son of a prince.

"How handsome these boys are, and how intelligent!" King Nebuchadnezzar had remarked. "They'll be fine men one day. But I am their king, and I can train them to become what I like. I want them to forget that they are Jews. From now on they must be Babylonians."

So Daniel and his three friends were taught to speak the king's language instead of Hebrew. They were given lessons in science and philosophy by the wise men of Babylon. The king himself liked to keep an eye on them and, to show the boys how pleased he was with their progress, he ordered that the best food and drink from his table should be brought to them.

"Tell them that the meat and the wine are a personal present from me," he said.

When the servants brought the food to the boys they gently pushed it away. Since the earliest days of Jewish history their religion had forbidden them to eat certain kinds of food, or to drink any wine.

"Do you think," said Daniel, "that we could have fruit and vegetables and water instead?"

The head of the king's household, was amazed. "What!" he cried. "If you don't eat this meat you'll starve. You will look pale and ill, and the king will kill me for it!"

"Let us try it for ten days," Daniel replied. "Give us fruit and vegetables to eat. You will see that we look just as healthy as the children who eat your meat."

So the steward, who liked the boys, agreed. When the ten days were over he found that, far from looking starved, the boys were healthier than the other children. From then on they were allowed to eat what they liked, and God was pleased with them.

At the end of their three-year schooling at court Nebuchadnezzar tested them on all that they had learned. He found that they knew more than any of his magicians and wise men, and he promoted them to be his advisers at court.

All went well with them until the day they refused to bow down to the idol. They alone had defied the king, and their punishment was to serve as a warning to others.

"Let them die!" exclaimed the king. "Throw them into the furnace!"

The king ordered the fires in the furnace to be stoked hotter than ever before. The king's guards bound Shadrach, Meshach and Abed-nego. Then they led them up to the furnace and threw them inside. The heat was so great that the guards themselves were burned to death by the flames.

The fire leaped up over the three young men as they raised their arms to heaven. The flames licked their bodies and roared around them. Shadrach, Meshach and Abed-nego stood in the middle of the furnace, wrapped around by flames, but they remained completely unharmed and quite calm.

[176]

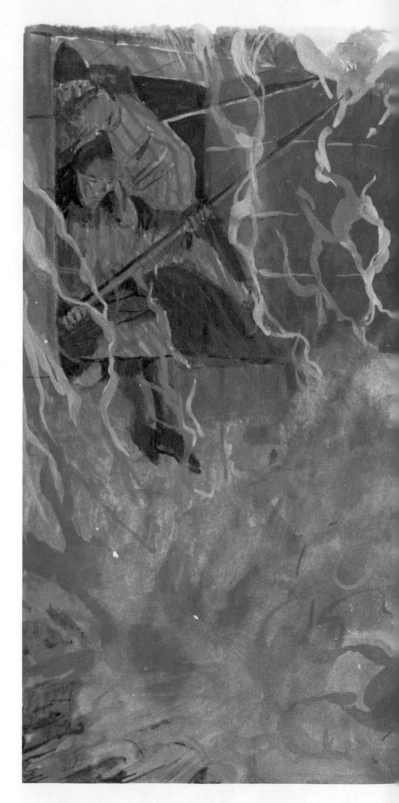

Nebuchadnezzar watched the spectacle with amazement. He called to his counsellors:

"Did we not throw three men, bound with ropes, into the fire?"

"We did, my lord," they replied.

"But I can see four men, unbound, walking in it! I can see them clearly—and the

fourth man looks like an angel or a god!"

Nebuchadnezzar walked up to the furnace and called through the flames:

"Come out, you servants of God!"

Shadrach, Meshach and Abed-nego walked out through the furnace's closed gates. The ropes that had bound them were gone. A great crowd of people gathered around them to see what sort of men these were, who could survive being thrown into the flames. Not a hair on their heads was singed, and there was not even the smell of smoke on their clothes.

Nebuchadnezzar raised his arms.

"Blessed be the God of Shadrach, Meshach and Abed-nego!" he cried.

The Interpretation and Fulfilment of the Dream

KING NEBUCHADNEZZAR was again troubled by a dream. He woke from it with terror in his heart. Then the nightmare began to spread into his waking hours, and haunt him.

He called together the wise men and magicians of Babylon. They listened to him in silence, but not one of them could explain the dream. They went away puzzled and afraid.

Then the king called for Daniel and told him his dream.

"This is what I saw," he said. "I saw a great tree with its roots in the middle of the earth. The tree grew bigger and more powerful; its top reached into the sky and seemed to touch it. From every corner of the earth the tree could be seen. Its boughs and its leaves were beautiful and it was heavy with fruit. Everybody ate its fruit. The tree gave shelter to wild beasts under its boughs, and birds built their nests in its branches. Everything that is alive found shelter and food there.

"But while I looked on, a messenger from God came down from heaven. 'Cut down

the tree,' he cried, 'scatter the fruit, strip the branches bare of leaves. Let the wild beasts flee from its shelter, and the birds from its branches. Leave the stump and the roots of the tree in the soil. Tie it together with an iron ring, and let the grass grow around it and the dew from heaven fall on it!'"

The king turned to Daniel. "Tell me what the dream means. I know you can, because you have the spirit of God in you, which tells you the truth."

"My lord," Daniel answered, "your dream fills me with sadness. The tree which you saw grow until it reached into the sky, which could be seen from the furthest corner of the earth, whose leaves and fruit gave shelter and fruit to everyone – that tree is you. But in your pride you will be struck down with madness, and become an example to all men. The God who holds you in his power will bring you low, so that you may learn that he is greater than any earthly king and can raise up and throw down whoever he wants to."

The king was not pleased to hear Daniel's words and as the months passed, he gradually forgot them. One day he was looking down on the roofs of Babylon. His pride at his own power and wealth rose in him, and knew no bounds. At that moment he was struck down with madness. His mind snapped; he became insane and could no longer rule as king. He was thrown out of the city and lived, like an animal, in the wild, eating grass and lying in the open until his hair grew long like a goat's and his nails were like an eagle's talons.

Twelve years passed, and then, equally suddenly, Nebuchadnezzar was healed. He began to praise God, the king of kings. His madness left him and he was sane again. He became king once more, a better and a humbler man, who ruled justly and believed in the power of God to the end of his days.

The Writing on the Wall

WHEN Nebuchadnezzar died his son, Belshazzar, reigned in his place. One day the new king gave a feast for all the princes and nobles of his kingdom. He called for wine and then for more; soon, he began to grow drunk.

"Fetch me the drinking cups of the Jews," he called to his servants. "The ones my father Nebuchadnezzar took from the altars of their Temple. We will drink from them tonight."

So the holy vessels stolen from the Temple of God in Jerusalem were brought in, and filled with wine. The goblets and bowls were handed to Belshazzar's courtiers and his concubines, and they drank from them. The king held up his goblet of hammered gold.

"Let us praise the god of gold!" he called. The men and women around him took up the cry. They praised the gods of silver, of bronze and of iron, and drank to them out of the sacred cups. Then they praised the gods of wood and of stone, and drank yet again.

Suddenly the words the king was about to speak died away on his lips. On the wall opposite him there appeared a hand. Its fingers began to move, and it wrote four words. Then it faded away, but the writing did not. The king's face paled and his body shook with fear.

"What does it mean?" he asked. But no one could tell him. He called loudly for his magicians and wise men.

"Whoever can read this writing and interpret it for me," he said, "will be rewarded with riches and honour."

The wise men looked for a long time at the writing on the wall, but they could neither read it nor interpret it. Then the queen came into the hall.

"Why do you look so pale, my lord?" she asked. "I know of a man who can tell you the meaning of the words. His name is Daniel and he is a Jew. He has often in the past read omens for your father."

Belshazzar sent for Daniel. He pointed to the writing on the wall.

"Tell me what it means," he said, "and I will reward you with gold and honour."

"Keep your gold and your honour, my lord," Daniel replied. "The hand you saw was the hand of God. In your pride you drank out of the holiest vessels of God's Temple, and you defiled them. You have praised the gods of silver and of gold, but you have not spoken of the glory of the one God who has all men in his keeping. The writing on the wall is this: *mene mene tekel u-pharsin*. It means that the days of your kingdom are numbered, and that it will soon fall. It means that God has judged your actions and found them unworthy of you. It means that your enemies the Medes and the Persians will divide your kingdom between them."

Daniel spoke the truth. Before the night was over the king of the Medes attacked Babylon, killed Belshazzar and made his lost kingdom into part of the Median Empire.

Daniel in the Lions' Den

DANIEL knew more and was wiser than any man in Babylon. Darius the Great, the king of the Medes and the Persians, sent for him and said:

"I am going to put new governors in my provinces—there will be 120 of them. They will answer to three presidents. I want you to be their chief. There will be no one in the land more powerful than you, except myself."

To Darius it did not matter that Daniel was not a Babylonian but a Jew—a stranger in the land. But it did matter to the princes, governors and presidents who all had to answer to Daniel. They were jealous because he had more power than they, and they began to hate him. So they started to look about them for a way of removing him from the king's favour, of destroying him completely.

But Daniel was an honourable man and did his work well; it was difficult to find anything that could be held against him. He was the king's favourite, and rarely left his master.

"He never seems to break the law," his enemies said, "and he does everything the king commands. But he is a Jew, and his obedience to his God is even greater than his obedience to the king. We will set a trap for him that will lead to his death."

The princes, presidents and governors went to Darius. They bowed low to him, and then they said:

"King Darius, live for ever! May your power over the people never grow less. We have drawn up a law to test the good will and loyalty of your people here in Babylon. You must forbid everyone to pray to any god or ask a favour of any power but your

own. If a man wants something, he must ask the king and the king alone."

"Why do you want to make this law?" the king said to them.

"Because there are some people in Babylon who are in touch with your enemies and they may betray you," his advisers replied.

"I think it would be sufficient to make

this law last only for the next 30 days," Darius suggested. "That should give us time to find out if any man is not loyal to us."

This did not worry the princes because they knew they could trap Daniel with the law in less than a day. "How will you punish anyone who disobeys the law?" one of them asked the king.

"What would you suggest?" Darius asked.

"We say that any man who breaks this law –which is a law of the Medes and Persians and therefore can never be changed–should die by being thrown to the lions," the prince answered. Like other rich men, the king kept lions in a pit in his gardens, so that he could set them free when he wanted to, and hunt them for sport.

So Darius, who believed in the good faith of his advisers, signed the order, and his words became law.

When Daniel heard about the king's new law he was deeply distressed, because he knew he would have to break it, even if it cost him his life. He went home to his house and slowly climbed the flight of stairs outside it to the room on the top of the flat roof where he prayed to God. Every Jewish house had a room set aside where men went three times each day to pray.

Daniel opened the windows and looked westwards, towards Jerusalem. He remembered that he was an exile in a foreign land, that his people had been banished from their country because they had angered God.

"Forgive us, Lord," he prayed. "Make us better people. Help us to understand you."

Daniel's enemies had gathered around the house. They knew where the room was in which he said his prayers to God, and when they saw him at the window, they knew they had enough evidence to trap him.

They hurried to the king. "Didn't you sign an order, my lord, saying that any man who prayed to anyone other than yourself in the next 30 days would be thrown to the lions?" they asked.

"I did," said the king.

"We have found a man who has broken the order; he has disobeyed the king's command. He must die."

"He must," the king agreed. "What is his name?"

"His name is Daniel, and he is one of the Jews."

Darius was dismayed. Daniel was his most trusted servant; he knew that he was more loyal than all the princes in the land. He looked for a way to save him, but could find

none. In the evening Daniel's enemies returned to the palace.

"Remember," they warned, "that the king's word is law. It is the law of the Medes and Persians, which may never be changed."

It seemed to Darius that he had no choice. Sadly, he ordered Daniel to be arrested. When his friend and adviser was brought to him in chains, he tried to bring him hope.

"You serve your God so faithfully, Daniel," he said. "Surely he will save you."

Daniel was led to the side of the pit. The lions were prowling about below, roaring because they were hungry. The king's guards threw Daniel into the pit and rolled a stone over the top to cover it. The king himself sealed the stone with the royal seal, so that no one could break in and rescue Daniel. Then he went back to the palace and prayed all night for his friend.

At sunrise he returned to the pit, broke the seals and rolled back the stone. He was trembling.

"Are you there, Daniel?" he called out.

"Yes, my lord. My God has saved me. I am alive and well. The lions are sleeping around me."

The king was overjoyed. "Oh, Daniel, my friend," he cried. "Praised be your God!"

Then he gave orders that all his people should gather to see the miracle. Daniel was lifted out of the pit and brought to the king. There was not a scratch on him. The lions had not touched Daniel because he had put his trust in God. But when the wicked advisers were thrown into the pit to punish them, the lions leaped on them at once and tore them to pieces, and ate them.

So Darius issued a new decree. It read:

"Throughout my lands men must worship the God of Daniel, for he is the only true God. His power will never end. He is a saviour and a worker of wonders in heaven and on earth, because he has brought his servant Daniel safely out of the lions' den."

Rebuilding the Temple

WHEN Cyrus became emperor of Persia and king of Babylon he gave the Jews their freedom, after half a century of slavery. They were free to return to Judah and its capital, Jerusalem.

Thousands of men and women gathered together for the long journey back. With them Cyrus sent back all the treasures of gold and silver that Nebuchadnezzar had brought from the Temple of God; every candlestick, pitcher and bowl that had been taken was given back.

When the Babylonian Jews reached Jerusalem they first built a small altar to God, and then they celebrated the gathering in of the harvest, or feast of the Tabernacles. They began to repair the city, which was in ruins, as best they could. They sowed the fields with grain and gathered the harvest, but they built no Temple.

Years went by and still no Temple was built. At last two prophets, Haggai and Zechaniah, appeared among the people.

"What are you waiting for?" they asked. "God is with you. He will give you power and riches, and Israel will be great again. The Persian king has promised us his support if we rebuild the Temple."

So the people set to work. It took them about four years to complete it, and the first feast that was celebrated in the new Temple was the Passover. Appropriately, it was the feast of thanksgiving, the reminder of the Jews' release from captivity.

The Rebuilding of the Wall

THE Temple was rebuilt, but all around it the walls of the city lay in ruins. Other tribes had settled in Jerusalem while the Jews were in Babylon, and the city had become a small province of the Persian Empire.

The years passed and Jerusalem remained a city without walls to defend it. Its people were too poor and confused to build the walls and make Jerusalem a proud city once again. Many of the leading Jews were still living in other lands in the cities where their enemies had taken them years before. They had risen to positions of importance, and had won the friendship of kings.

One such man was Nehemiah. He had become the cup bearer to the king of Persia, and his master liked him. One day, as the king and queen were sitting at table the king noticed that something about Nehemiah had changed.

"What is it?" he asked. "You don't seem to be ill. Are you unhappy?"

"Yes, my lord," replied the cup bearer. "My brother Hanani is here on a visit. He has come from Jerusalem, and he says that our city there is falling down. The walls that King Nebuchadnezzar destroyed have still not been rebuilt. May I go, my lord, to build them up again?"

"It depends how long you will be away," replied the king. So Nehemiah set a date for

his return and the king agreed to let him go. Then Nehemiah made some more requests.

"Will you give me a pass, my lord, that will take me through your provinces? And a letter to Asaph, the keeper of your forests? I will need much timber to build the gates and the walls."

The king gave him everything he asked for.

When Nehemiah arrived in Jerusalem, he found that the local governor and his officers did not want the city walls rebuilt and their power over the city taken away. They put every kind of difficulty in his way.

At first Nehemiah began his work in secret, at night. With the help of other Jews the new walls and the gates began to take shape.

"Are you planning a rebellion?" the Arabs and the Ammonites living in the city asked them.

"No," answered Nehemiah. "Our God wants us to do this and is helping us. It is none of your business, anyway. Not one of you has any claim or right to live in Jerusalem."

The others jeered. "What sort of wall is this anyway?" they called out. "If a fox ran along the top of it, it would collapse under his weight!"

They began to attack the Jewish workers and threatened to kill them. Nehemiah ordered his men to report to work with a tool in one hand and a weapon in the other. Half of them would mount guard while the others carried bricks and mortar for the walls.

In turn, each of the gates that led into Jerusalem was rebuilt and its massive doors set in place. They were barred and bolted. Gradually, great walls rose between the gates until at last the city stood safe and protected once more by its circle of strong walls, as it had in the time of King David.

The Story of Esther

THERE was once a mighty king of Persia whose empire stretched from India to Africa. He had everything he wanted, and more besides. One day the king held a great banquet. It lasted for seven days and seven nights, and the wine flowed freely. On the seventh day the king sent for his queen, Vashti, so that she might show her beauty to his men. But the queen refused, and the king was so angry that he banished her.

He let it be known that he was looking for a new queen. The loveliest girls in the kingdom were brought to his harem by their willing fathers and spent twelve months there, learning how to make themselves beautiful enough to please the king. When each girl had been there a full year the king had her brought to him in the evening so that he could sleep with her, and taken away again in the morning. In this way he found Esther, a Jewish girl, who pleased him so much that he made her queen in Vashti's place.

Now Esther's guardian was a Jew called Mordecai. One day he overheard two courtiers, the keepers of the threshold, plotting to kill their master. Mordecai told Esther, who warned the king, and the two men were hanged.

"Write all this down," said the king, "and mention the name of Mordecai, who discovered the plot."

Next, the king appointed a man as his adviser who was called Haman. Haman was a proud and ambitious man, who hated all Jews. Most of all he hated Mordecai, because Mordecai would not kneel to him as others did.

Haman persuaded the king to have every

Jew in Persia murdered, and they fixed a day, the day of Pur, when the massacre would take place.

When Mordecai told Esther about Haman's order she was afraid for her people. Putting on her royal robes she risked her life by appearing before the king when he had not sent for her. But he was so struck by her beauty that he made her welcome and offered to give her anything she wanted.

"Please dine with me tonight in my rooms," was Esther's request, "and bring Haman with you."

The king was pleased, and over their wine that night he again told Esther he would grant her whatever she wished. "Take half my kingdom, if you like," he told her.

But Esther had a different favour to ask.

"My lord, do you remember how Mordecai, my uncle, once saved your life? He is a Jew, and so am I. Now Haman your servant wants to kill him and me and all our people. We are innocent. Spare us, my lord!"

The king at once ordered Haman to be taken out and hanged. In his place he appointed Mordecai as his adviser. The old man was given splendid robes and a crown of gold. His first act was to order that the day of killing that Haman had ordered at the time of Pur should still take place. It should be remembered as the day of vengeance against the enemies of the Jews.

With the king's permission the Jews in every city united. They killed every man, woman and child who hated them, and took their possessions. The day of Pur became a day for feasting and joy and triumph, to be remembered by the Jewish people every year for all time as the festival of Purim.

God's Testing of Job

AGOOD man once lived in the land of Uz, and his name was Job. He loved God and used to pray to him every day before he went out to work on his farm. He was helped in everything he did by his sons and daughters, and was loved and respected by all.

"It's all very well to be good like Job when everything is going well," scoffed Satan, the Devil, to God, "but he'd soon lose courage if things went wrong with him. Let's say if he lost all his children, or his farm, or if he fell really ill—he wouldn't love you then!"

So God decided to test Job.

He let all these things happen to him, and, just as Satan had predicted, Job grew bitter and angry. His friends tried to tell him why God allows us to feel pain—to make us see things more clearly, to make us less proud, to make us into stronger people.

Then God himself spoke to Job. He reminded him that men know so little about life, let alone about anything that goes on beyond it. Job was impatient.

"But why, why, *why*, Lord?" he asked.

Then God stopped talking and appeared before him. Now Job no longer needed the answers. He was filled with peace, and with the fullness and glory of God's presence.

Jonah and the Whale

JONAH was going about his daily work when God spoke to him.

"Jonah," he said. "I want you to go to Nineveh. The people there are wicked. Tell them that their city and everything in it will be destroyed within 40 days."

"Why choose me, Lord?" Jonah replied in dismay. "Why should I, an ordinary Jew in Israel, go to preach about God to people I don't know, who live far away, and who are not even Jews and don't believe in you? Besides, you are a kind and merciful God; you would never wipe out a whole city like that."

He decided not to go. But he was afraid of God's anger, and tried to escape by going on board a ship bound for Tarshish, in the opposite direction to Nineveh. The ship set sail and Jonah fell asleep in the hold.

Suddenly a great storm blew up and the captain shook Jonah awake.

"Come," he said. "Perhaps it's your God who is angry with us." Jonah prayed, but the storm grew worse. "Look," he said to the sailors, "I know it's my fault; you had better throw me overboard."

The sailors did not want to do that, so they rowed hard, trying to get back to land.

But the hurricane blew more fiercely than ever, so they dropped Jonah overboard.

The winds died down at once. At first Jonah floated on the waves, but not for long. A great fish, like a whale, came and swallowed him up, and for three days and three nights he lay inside its belly. Then the fish spat him out, safe, onto the beach.

Again God commanded Jonah to go to Nineveh, and this time he obeyed at once. He arrived at the great city and walked through the streets, calling out, "In 40 days Nineveh will be destroyed!"

The people who heard him were afraid, for they believed in God's power. They took Jonah to the king, and the king ordered that every man and woman in the city should pray for forgiveness for their wickedness and resolve to begin a new life. God was pleased with their prayers and spared Nineveh.

Jonah, however, was angry with God. He felt that he had been made to look a fool. "I knew all along that you wouldn't kill them," he grumbled.

He went out into the desert and sat down. The sun grew hot and uncomfortable, so God made a tree grow over him to give him shade. The next day the tree withered and died and the sun scorched Jonah until he began to feel very ill.

"I'm sorry for that tree; it lived such a short time," said Jonah to himself. "I wish I were dead too."

Then God spoke gently to him. "If you feel sorry for this tree, which you neither planted nor watered, how much more sorry I would have been, to have had to destroy Nineveh. My love is greater than yours. I forgive those who repent, and I bring comfort to all men."

The New Testament

The New Testament

CONTENTS

Elizabeth and Zacharias   198

An Angel Visits Mary   199

The Birth of John   200

The Birth of Jesus   201

The Visit of the Wise Men   204

The Prophecy of Simeon   206

The Flight into Egypt   207

Jesus and the Teachers   209

John the Baptist Baptizes Jesus   210

The Temptation in the Wilderness   212

Jesus in Galilee   214

The Marriage at Cana   216

Jesus Heals the Leper and the
    Soldier's Servant   218

Jesus Heals the Paralyzed Man   220

Jesus Explains — 221

The Choosing of the Twelve Apostles — 222

The Sermon on the Mount — 224

Jesus Calms the Storm — 226

Jesus Heals a Madman — 228

Jairus's Daughter — 229

The Death of John the Baptist — 230

The Parables — 232

Jesus and the Children — 242

The Feeding of the Five Thousand — 244

Jesus Walks on the Water — 246

Jesus Foretells the Crucifixion — 248

The Journey to Jerusalem — 250

Jesus Visits the Home of Mary and Martha — 251

Lazarus Is Brought Back to Life — 253

Jesus' Enemies Plot to Kill Him — 254

Jesus Warns the Disciples of What Lies Ahead — 256

The Entry into Jerusalem 257

The Withered Fig Tree 259

Jesus Drives the Money Changers
out of the Temple 260

Jesus Answers the Sadducees
and the Pharisees 262

The Widow's Gift 263

Jesus Describes the Day of Judgment 264

Judas Plots Against Jesus 265

The Last Supper 266

Jesus Predicts His Betrayal 268

Jesus Prays in the Garden of Gethsemane 269

The Betrayal 271

Peter Disowns Jesus 272

The Trial and the Mockery 273

The Crucifixion 275

The Burial 278

The Resurrection 280

The Disciples See Jesus 282

Thomas Doubts 283

Jesus at the Sea of Galilee 284

The Ascent into Heaven 285

The Beginning of the Church in Jerusalem 286

The Healing of the Lame Beggar 287

The First Martyr 288

The Conversion of Paul and His Escape 289

The Teaching of Peter and His Escape 292

Paul's First Journey 294

Paul's Second Journey 296

Paul's Third Journey 297

Paul in Jerusalem and Rome 298

Paul's Last Years 301

The Letters of Peter 302

The Vision of John 303

Elizabeth and Zacharias

CENTURIES passed. The country of Judah was conquered yet again and became part of the Roman Empire. It was called Judaea and remained a separate kingdom, ruled by a Jewish king named Herod. The real power, however, was in the hands of the Roman governor.

During Herod's reign a priest lived in Judaea whose name was Zacharias. He and his wife Elizabeth loved God and obeyed his commandments, but they were sad because they had no child. "Oh God, give us a son," they prayed.

One day Zacharias was taking part in a service in the Temple at Jerusalem when an angel appeared.

"Do not be afraid, Zacharias," the angel said. "God has heard your prayer. You will have a son and you will call him John. He will be a great teacher and a man of God. He will be filled with the spirit of the prophet Elijah; he will bring the people back to God and prepare for the coming of our Lord."

"How can this be?" Zacharias asked. "We are too old to have a son."

"I am Gabriel," the angel replied, "and God has sent me. But because you doubt his word you will be struck dumb and you will remain so until the things I have told you come true."

When Zacharias came home, he could not tell Elizabeth about his vision because he was dumb. But Elizabeth told him:

"We are going to have a child. God has arranged it—he has heard our prayers."

An Angel Visits Mary

A FEW months later God sent the angel Gabriel to the town of Nazareth in Galilee, to visit a young girl. She had been promised in marriage to a man named Joseph, who was descended from the family of King David. The girl's name was Mary.

The angel appeared to her and said, "Greetings, Mary, God's blessing is on you." When Mary saw the angel and heard what he said she was filled with wonder and unease.

"Do not be afraid, Mary," the angel continued, "God loves you; he has filled you with his grace. You will have a child, a son whom you will call Jesus. He will be great, and people will call him the Son of the Highest. God will give him the throne of his forefather David, and he will reign over Israel for ever. His kingdom will never cease to exist."

"How can this be?" asked Mary. "I have never slept with a man."

The angel Gabriel replied, "The Holy Spirit of God is with you; God will take possession of you. And because of this, the holy child that will be born from your body will be called the Son of God."

The angel went on, "Through God's will your cousin Elizabeth will also have a son. You know she could not have children before and seemed too old to bear any now, but she will give birth before you. God can make everything possible."

Mary said, "I am God's servant. May everything happen just as you have said."

The Birth of John

MARY hurried to visit Elizabeth, who was staying in a town in the hills. When her cousin saw her coming she was suddenly filled with the spirit of God. She ran to welcome Mary and the two women embraced.

"You are blessed among women," Elizabeth told her cousin, "and so is your child! You are the mother of our Lord, and you fill my house with light. Why, when you greeted me just now, my child leaped for joy inside me. How important it is for a woman to believe in God, for you and I are proof that he can make wonderful things happen!"

In time a son was born to Elizabeth. When he was eight days old he was taken to be circumcized, which was–and still is–the custom of the Jews, and be given a name.

"Of course you will call him Zacharias, after his father," the people said.

The old man could not speak, except by signs, but he remembered the angel's words. They brought him a slate and he wrote on it:

"His name is John."

Immediately Zacharias could speak again and he cried: "Praise God! This child will be a prophet of the Lord who will free us, and rescue us from our enemies. He will go first to prepare the way for him. He will tell the people that their sins are forgiven and that they are saved. Then God in his mercy will send us a light. It will shine on everyone who feels lost and afraid, or frightened of dying, and guide us all towards peace."

The Birth of Jesus

THE months passed from spring to summer, and then to autumn. The child that Mary carried slept in her and grew. Winter came, and Mary's body was heavy and full. It was time for her child to be born.

Now that Judaea was part of the Roman Empire Mary and Joseph had to obey the laws of Rome. "Every man and woman who lives in our lands must pay tax," went the proclamation of the Emperor Augustus. "A new register will be drawn up, on which the name of every citizen is written. The Emperor wants a complete record of his people."

When King Herod heard this command, he ordered everyone in his kingdom to return to the place of their birth to be put on the register. Because Joseph belonged to the family of David, he had to leave Nazareth where he lived and worked, and go back to Bethlehem, which lay some 70 miles to the south.

As his wife, Mary had to go too, although her child was expected any day. Together they set off on their mule over the hills to Bethlehem. In the evening they arrived in the city, and tried to find somewhere to stay. But Joseph was poor and the streets were crowded with people.

"Go away," the people said. "Bethlehem is full of outsiders like you, coming in from the hills and valleys to be registered." They looked at Mary, who sat tired and heavy on the mule. "Move off," they said, and sent her away.

Night had fallen, and Joseph wrapped his cloak around Mary and led her down the street. He knocked at the door of another house. A woman opened it a crack to look at them. "No room," she said firmly, and shut the door in their faces.

Now Mary slipped gently off the mule, because it too was tired. They walked on until they came to an inn. Lamps burned in every window and the rooms inside were full of people eating and drinking. Horses, camels and donkeys stood munching their hay in the courtyard. Joseph knocked on the door. The landlord opened it.

"No room at the inn!" he called out, and waved them away. As they moved on, the light from the door fell on Mary.

"You can sleep in the stable, if you like. The straw there is fresh," the landlord called after her.

So Mary made a bed for herself in the sweet-smelling hay. And there, with the ox and the donkey beside her, she gave birth to her son. She wrapped him up well and laid him in a manger filled with hay. She called him Jesus, which means, "God Saves".

That night the words of the prophet Isaiah came true:

"*For unto us a child is born; unto us a son is given;*
And the government shall be upon his shoulders,
And his name shall be
Wonderful, Counsellor, the Prince of Peace,
The Mighty God, The Everlasting Father."

In the hills around Bethlehem shepherds were out in the fields, taking care of their flocks during the night. Suddenly an angel appeared to them, and the glory of God shone around them. The shepherds were terrified because there was so much light.

"Don't be afraid," the angel said to them. "I have good news for you – tonight a Saviour has been born to you in Bethlehem, the city of David. His name is Christ, the Lord."

Then the light increased so that its splendour lit up the fields as if it was day, and the sky was filled with the angels of God. Their voices rose like the wind and swept over the hills and valleys as they sang:

"Glory to God in the highest, and on earth peace, good will towards men!"

Then the light and the music gradually

faded away and the shepherds said to one another:

"Come, let's go to Bethlehem and see the holy thing that has happened there!"

They ran down into the town and came to the stable where Mary and Joseph were resting. They saw the baby sleeping in the manger, and kneeled down and worshipped it.

Then they went out and told the people of Bethlehem what had happened, and everyone was astonished.

Mary treasured all these memories and thought about them often as Jesus grew up.

The Visit of the Wise Men

THE people of Judaea did not realize that a star had risen over Bethlehem. They did not notice that the nights were no longer dark, that a new star, brighter than any other had appeared in the sky, directly above the stable where Jesus had been born.

King Herod himself first heard of the star through strangers when three wise men came to visit him from the East.

"What is this light that has appeared over your country?" they asked. "We have noticed a new star in heaven. It does not move like the other stars, but stays fixed in place above one spot in Judaea."

Herod looked at the wise men. They were old, and obviously skilled at understanding and interpreting the movements of stars and their meanings. But he could not understand what they were talking about. Their next question took him quite by surprise.

"Where is this child who is born to be king of the Jews?" they asked.

"Born to be *what*?" he exclaimed.

"King of the Jews. We think he is the Messiah, the Saviour that all the world is waiting for. That is why we are here."

Herod did not like the idea at all. *He* was king of the Jews and he wanted no one to take his place. He called for his high priests and scholars.

"What do you know about a new king of Judaea?" he asked. "Is it true that we are to have a Messiah?"

"Yes, my lord, it is true. The writings of the prophets say so," the priests replied.

"When? Where?" the king demanded.

One of the scholars came forward. "It's all written down in the book of the prophet Micah, sir," he said. "It's to happen in Bethlehem. This is how Micah puts it—the language is old-fashioned but the meaning is clear—'*And thou Bethlehem, in the land of Judah, art not the least among the princes of Judah: for out of thee shall come a Government that shall rule my people Israel.*'"

Herod had heard enough. He turned to the strangers. "Find this king," he said. "And come back and tell me where he is.

I want to go and—er—worship him too."

The wise men set out and once again the star stood out, brilliantly clear, in the eastern sky. Its light drew them onwards, and they followed it until over Bethlehem it seemed to stand still.

There they found Mary and Joseph, and the baby Jesus, lying in the hay. They knew this was the king they had come so far to find, and they fell down on their knees and worshipped him.

Then each man reached into his saddle bags and drew out the present he had brought. Gently they laid their gifts in the hay around the child.

They gave gold, which was a gift for kings, and frankincense, which was burned on the altar of God. And they gave myrrh, which was used in those days to help preserve men's bodies after death.

The Prophecy of Simeon

An old man called Simeon lived in Jerusalem. "Please, God," he prayed, "let me see the Messiah just once. Then I shall be able to die in peace."

"Go to the Temple, Simeon," God said to him, "and you will find him there."

That same day Mary had taken Jesus to the Temple to present him to God. As was customary among the Jews, she and Joseph offered a pair of turtle doves in exchange for their first-born son, as a thanksgiving to God.

When Simeon saw Mary carrying her child he came towards her.

"Blessed be God," he said, and took the baby from her. He held Jesus in his arms and said softly:

"Lord, now your servant can die in peace, for his prayer has been heard. My eyes have seen the salvation that will come to all men. The light that now shines on earth will bring glory to your people Israel."

Then he turned to Mary, who was standing amazed at his words, and said, as he put the baby back into her arms:

"Your child will make many men great and will cause some to fall. But there will be people who will not believe in him, and your heart will be pierced with sorrow."

When Mary and Joseph had finished making their offering to God, they went back to Bethlehem with their baby.

The Flight into Egypt

"Do not tell King Herod where to find Jesus," God said to the wise men in a dream, "And do not go back the way you came. Leave Israel secretly."

The wise men obeyed promptly; by the time Herod's spies realized what had happened, they were far away.

Then Joseph, too, received a message from God. An angel appeared to him in a dream and said:

"Joseph, you are in great danger. Herod wants to kill the child. He is looking for you everywhere. Take Mary and the baby and flee with them to Egypt. Stay there until I tell you to return. Hurry!"

Joseph woke up. Everything seemed quiet around him. Then somewhere a dog barked. He rose quickly and slipped on his sandals. Then he shook Mary gently.

"Wake up, Mary!" he said. "We must escape before King Herod finds us!"

"May God be with us," said Mary, and wrapped Jesus in her cloak.

They left Bethlehem as they had come,

riding on a mule. But this time Mary carried the child in her arms, and the night seemed to fold itself around them and hide them from men's eyes. By sunrise they were far away to the south, and when they had crossed the border into Egypt they knew they were safe.

Herod, meanwhile, was waiting impatiently for the wise men to return. As the days and weeks passed, his impatience changed to suspicion. At last he sent his spies to hunt for them.

"Why, they've been gone a long time, now!" the people in Bethlehem said. "They went somewhere in that direction," and they waved towards the eastern hills.

When Herod heard how he had been tricked he fell into a fury. He tried to remember exactly what it was that the wise men had said. They had mentioned a child king, and they had gone to Bethlehem.

He was determined to resist any claim to his throne, but he had no idea where to find the child that the wise men had said would be king. He did not even know its name. He only knew that it lived in Bethlehem and could not be more than two years old. In a fit of jealous fear he commanded that all children in Bethlehem under two years of age should be killed.

His soldiers marched into the town, snatched the terrified children from their mothers' arms and killed every one of them. A terrible wailing filled the air, as the mothers of Bethlehem sat down in the streets with their dead babies in their arms, mourning and weeping for the children they had lost.

Time passed. Another king sat on the throne of Judaea. Mary and Joseph were still living in Egypt, and Jesus had grown into a young boy. Then an angel came to Joseph in a dream and said, "Go back to Israel, for Herod the King is dead." So they returned to Israel, and settled in Nazareth.

Jesus and the Teachers

WHEN Jesus was twelve years old he went with his parents to Jerusalem. It was their habit to make a pilgrimage there every year to give thanks to God at the feast of the Passover. He joined in offering the sacrifice of lamb, honey and wine, and ate the crisp, hard, unleavened bread that reminded the Jews of their flight from Egypt.

When the festival was over his parents set out to go home again to Nazareth.

"Where is Jesus?" Mary asked.

"He must have gone ahead with the other pilgrims," she was told.

But when they looked for Jesus among the crowds of pilgrims they could not find him. Deeply worried, Mary and Joseph hurried back to Jerusalem. They spent three days looking in all the bazaars and markets, but they could not find him. Then they went to the Temple, their last hope.

"There he is, look, in Solomon's Porch!" cried Joseph. Jesus was sitting among the scholars who taught in the Temple, as if he were one of them. He was asking them questions and listening to their answers, and everyone who heard him was amazed at his wisdom.

"My son, what are you doing?" Mary cried. "We have been so worried about you!"

Calmly and gently Jesus replied, "Why did you look for me? Didn't you know that I was bound to be in my father's house?"

Then he went back with them to Nazareth. As he grew older, he learned to become a carpenter. But it was obvious that God had given him special wisdom and grace, and everyone who knew him loved him.

John the Baptist Baptizes Jesus

For hundreds of years the Jews had been waiting for their Saviour to come. They were longing for someone to free them from Roman rule and from the hateful taxes they had to pay.

John was first to recognize that Jesus was the Saviour everyone was waiting for. He was Jesus' cousin, six months older than he, and as a priest's son he had been brought up to serve in the Temple in Jerusalem. He saw there how the rich ill-treated the poor, and he soon came to feel that God was not present in the Temple with its greedy, weak priests.

So John went into the desert, as Elijah had done. Like the prophet, he wore a rough camel-hair shirt and let his hair hang to his shoulders. He ate locusts and wild honey, and drank water from a goat skin he filled at desert wells. He lived in caves, waiting for God to speak to him.

One day he felt a great stillness lying over the hills. Then God said to him:

"Call the people of Israel; prepare them for the coming of their Lord."

John did not go to the towns; he began preaching where he was, in the desert. People came because they were curious, and stayed because they believed.

"Prepare!" he cried, "Prepare for the Kingdom of God! Stop offering sacrifices in the Temple; stop doing wrong to your neighbours!"

He baptized the people by dipping their bodies in the river Jordan, as a sign that everything wrong in them was washed away and they intended to try to live better lives in future and follow God's commandments.

"What do we do now?" the people asked.

"If you have two coats, give one to the man who has none," he replied. "If you have enough food, give half of it to those who are hungry."

Some tax collectors who had come to be baptized asked him, "What shall we do?"

"Be honest," he said. "Don't take money from others and keep it for yourselves."

Then some soldiers said to him, "And what about us?"

"Don't hurt other people," John replied, "and be content with your pay."

"Who are you, anyway?" they asked. "Are you Elijah? Or a prophet?"

John answered, "I am just a voice crying out in the desert. Prepare the way for the Lord! I am not the Saviour, the Christ. He will follow me and will be much more powerful than I. I baptize you with water, but he will baptize you with God's spirit and with fire. I am not worthy to touch even his shoes!"

When Jesus heard about John he left Nazareth and went to look for him. He found him on the banks of the Jordan and asked John to baptize him.

"That isn't right," John said to him. "It is I who should be baptized by you, for you are greater than I!"

Jesus answered, "It is God's will."

So John baptized Jesus in the river. As he was coming out of the water the skies seemed to open and he saw the spirit of God coming towards him in the shape of a dove. The voice of God said:

"You are my beloved Son, and I am very pleased with you."

The Temptation
in the Wilderness

GOD sent Jesus into the wilderness. He went alone into a desert far from the river Jordan where everything was dry and nothing grew.

There was silence around him. Elijah had once come here, and had wandered for 40 days and 40 nights over the stones and sand. Moses, before him, had counted 40 days go by as he spoke to God on Mount Horeb. Now it was Christ who stood in the waste land, and over whom 40 days and 40 nights were to pass.

He was hungry. Wherever he looked there was sand and there was stone. Even the wood that had once grown here had turned to stone.

He grew hungrier and he longed for bread. The wind blew waves of hot sand along the ground and threw it into his face.

"If you are the Son of God," the voice of the Devil said through the wind, "you can do anything you like. You can begin by turning these stones into bread!"

But Jesus replied, "Man does not live on bread alone; he needs the word of God."

Night fell, and the Devil carried Jesus to the holy city of Jerusalem. Here, from the highest ledge of the Temple, Jesus could see the domes and spires and the pools of water lying in their beauty below him.

"If you are the Son of God," the Devil whispered through the night wind, "you can throw yourself down into the city. The angels of God will hold you and will not let you fall. The time has come; show the people

[212]

that you are God. They will believe you and will make you king."

"No," said Jesus. "It is not for me to test God. He has sent me to share the pain and suffering of men."

The Devil took Jesus still higher. He took him to the highest mountain in the world. From here Jesus could see everything on earth from the beginning to the end of time. He saw the great kingdoms, the armies and the weapons of all mankind.

The Devil tempted him for the third time. "I can give you all these things," he said, "I will make you more powerful than any man has ever been. All you have to do is bow to me and worship me!"

Jesus cried out, "Go away, Satan–I cannot worship you; I cannot worship any-

thing but God. The Commandments tell us,
'*You shall worship God, and God alone*'!"

Then the Devil went away, and with him
went all the evil and darkness that had filled
the air. The angels of God came and brought
Jesus food and took care of him.

Jesus in Galilee

JESUS left his home in Nazareth and went to live in the countryside of Galilee. On one of his last days in the town he went into the synagogue to pray. (Synagogue was the name the Jews gave to the smaller temples where they met to offer prayers to God and hear God's words explained to them by the wise men who were called *Rabbis*.) Someone handed him the scroll of the prophet Isaiah and he read from it:

"The spirit of God is in me because he has anointed me; he has sent me to bring good news to the poor, to make the blind see and free men from captivity."

Jesus turned to the people and said, "Today, in this synagogue, the words of the prophet have come true!"

Everyone looked at him in amazement. Then they began to murmur: "But isn't this Joseph's son? The carpenter whom we all know?"

Jesus replied, "Yes, it is. A prophet is never welcomed in his own country. He must go out into the world and preach to strangers."

Then he walked out of the synagogue.

Why did Jesus not go to Jerusalem, the capital of Judaea? Because the priests and scholars there would have said, "We alone know the truth about God. We will not listen to a carpenter from Nazareth."

So he began his teaching and healing in the remote country district of Galilee.

"The time has come!" he called, as he walked through the wheatfields and vineyards that bordered the great lake known as the Sea of Galilee. "The Kingdom of God is near. Prepare yourselves, and be joyful!"

Once again Jesus walked along the banks of the river Jordan. He had come back to hear John, and to see the men whom John had gathered around him.

When John the Baptist saw Jesus coming, he pointed to him and said:

"There is the Lamb of God, whose sacrifice will wipe out the sins of the whole world."

Two men left John and ran to Jesus. He asked them:

"What do you want from me?"

"We want to hear you speak," they said.

"Come," said Jesus. So they stayed with him all that day, and the next morning one of them, who was called Andrew, brought his brother, who was a fisherman, to Jesus.

"You are Simon, son of John," Jesus said to the man. "From now on you shall be called Peter, which means 'the rock'."

Then Jesus met two more men, Philip and Nathanael, and said to them, "Follow me."

Nathanael kneeled down in front of Jesus. "You are indeed the Son of God, the King of Israel," he said.

The men who followed Jesus called him "Rabbi", because he was their teacher and they were his pupils, or disciples. They heard him speak about God and watched him heal the sick. They heard him teach in the synagogues, in the open fields, and by the Sea of Galilee. Some days so many people crowded around Jesus that he was in danger of being crushed. So he would take a boat out onto the lake and speak across the water to the people gathered on the shore.

"I have come to give men the life of God," he said to them one day. "It will come like living water into the world. It will heal them, and make them well again."

The Marriage at Cana

A MAN and a girl were getting married in Galilee. The wedding was being held in the village of Cana, and Jesus was one of the guests.

The feast had already gone on for several days. This was the last evening of the wedding, when the bride would be led to the bridegroom's house. She would be taken there at night, by torchlight, and she would be hidden from curious eyes by her long veil, with garlands of myrtle and orange blossom in her hair, and wound around her waist.

Jesus had brought his new disciples to the wedding with him. Mary his mother was there too; her husband Joseph had died many years before.

The family had invited everyone in the village to join in the feasting. A crowd of people filled the house and sat outside under the trees, eating and drinking and enjoying themselves.

Mary came up to Jesus quietly and waited until she could speak to him without being overheard.

"They have run out of wine," she said. "More people came to the wedding than were expected. The old wine's all gone and the new wine's turned sour."

"Can't they send out for more?" asked Jesus.

"No. You know how poor they are. All the money's gone on this food and the wine. They feel so ashamed."

"Why do you tell me all this?" asked Jesus. "The time when I can help has not come yet."

Jesus spoke these words gently. Mary still believed that he would help his friends.

"Do whatever he tells you to," she said to the servants.

They went back into the house. The wine-skins had run dry, but the guests did not know this yet. They were watching the drummer and the flute player, whose beat and shrill piping filled the air. The rhythm was getting faster; the people clapped in time to it while their feet pounded into the hard earth on the floor.

In the corner stood six large stone water jars, where it was customary for people to

wash their hands and feet as they entered the house. The spouts of the jars were stuffed with fresh green leaves, to keep the water cool. Jesus called to a servant:

"Fill these jars to the brim."

The servant drew the water from the well in the yard, and filled the jars.

"Now pour some off into smaller pitchers and take it to the chief guest," he said.

They carried the pitchers to the man and he drank from them, tasting each one in turn. He paused, then he laughed.

"Why, what wine is this?" he exclaimed, "I've never tasted anything like it!" He called across to the bridegroom:

"Other people serve their good wine first, and keep the poorer stuff to the end. But you have kept this wine, the best I've ever tasted, till now!"

The people were amazed. Everyone knew that the jars had been filled with water from the well. They looked at Jesus. Through the power God had given him he had turned water into wine. It was his first miracle.

Jesus Heals the Leper and the Soldier's Servant

ONE day a leper came to Jesus. In those days everyone was afraid of catching leprosy, so no one would go near a victim of this horrible disease to try to help him. Lepers had to warn people that they were coming by calling out, "Unclean! Unclean!" so that people could move well away. Lepers were not even allowed to worship in the Temple. The Jewish people believed that lepers were people who had done wrong in the past, and that God was punishing them for their sins.

As soon as Jesus saw the leper, his heart went out to him because he was suffering.

"I know you can heal me, Lord, if you want to," the man said, kneeling down.

Jesus stretched out his hand. "Indeed, I do want to," he said, and touched him.

"Be healed," he said, and immediately the terrifying sores vanished.

"Go now," Jesus told him, "and thank God in the Temple for your cure. Do not tell people about it; pray to God instead."

But the man could not help telling everyone he met about the new healer. People were filled with curiosity and followed Jesus

wherever he went, hoping to see a miracle happening before their own eyes. So Jesus left the crowds and went up into the hills to pray and to listen to God. Yet in time people came even here, to watch him.

Jesus went to a town in Galilee called Capernaum. There a Roman soldier came up to him and said:

"Sir, I have a servant at home who is very ill. He is a good man and I don't want him to die. Please, will you save him?"

"Take me to him," Jesus replied.

But the soldier hesitated. "I don't want to waste your time, sir," he said. "Just a word from you here and now would do." Jesus looked at him. The man went on:

"I'm nobody important—I just have a company of a hundred men under me, but I know the power of an order. Don't trouble to come all the way to my house. Just say the word, and my man will be cured."

"Your faith in me is great," said Jesus. "Most men want much more than just a word from me. They would not believe that I can cure men without touching or seeing them first. Well, I can. Go home now. Your servant will not die. I have healed him."

Jesus turned to the people around him. "You see," he said, "that man was a Gentile, a non-Jew, and he believed in me. The people of my own faith have not shown such trust. The time is coming when men from every country in the world will see the light of God and believe. But my own people here in Israel will not believe; the light will not shine through their darkness."

Jesus Heals the Paralyzed Man

A CROWD of people had gathered as usual while Jesus was preaching. Among them were a teacher and a priest, both Pharisees, members of a group of Jews who kept God's laws very strictly, and believed their way of worshipping was the only correct way. "Who is this man?" they asked. "What does he know about the laws of God? He's had no training from us!"

"He's talking about God," said a man beside them, "and about love and forgiveness. We've never heard anything like it!"

Four men came down the street, carrying a stretcher on which lay a paralyzed man.

"Take me to Jesus!" the sick man cried. With difficulty the men with the stretcher pushed their way through the crowd until they reached the open space where Jesus was standing, and laid their friend at his feet.

"Your sins are forgiven," said Jesus gently to the sick man.

"But that's impossible!" exclaimed the watching Pharisees. "Only God can forgive!"

Jesus heard them and replied, "I have the power to cure and to forgive. I can say, 'Your sins are forgiven,' just as easily as I can say, 'Stand up and walk'." He turned to the paralyzed man. "Stand up," he said, "and walk."

The man stretched and stood up. His body had been healed by Jesus, and his soul too.

Jesus Explains

THE people said to Jesus, "John the Baptist's disciples are always fasting and praying, just like the Pharisees do—why do your disciples eat and drink and enjoy themselves?"

Jesus answered, "Can you expect wedding guests to fast while they have the bridegroom with them? The time will come when the bridegroom will leave them; then will be the time to fast!"

He tried to explain in another way. "Nobody puts new wine into old wineskins. If he does, the new wine will burst the skins—the wine will be spilled and the skins ruined. New wine must be put into new wineskins.

"My teaching is new, like the wine, and so my disciples behave differently. People who are used to the old wine will go on drinking it. 'What was good enough before is good enough now,' they will say. They will not follow me to the Kingdom of God."

A Pharisee called Nicodemus said, "We know that God has sent you, Lord."

"Yes," replied Jesus, "I have come to bring men to God. But before they can enter his Kingdom, they must be born again."

"How is that possible?" asked Nicodemus, "We can't go back into our mothers' wombs!"

"I assure you," said Jesus, "that unless a man is born from water and the spirit he cannot come close to God. Your body is born from your mother's body, but only God's spirit can give birth to the spirit."

The Choosing of the Twelve Apostles

Jesus was walking by the Sea of Galilee early one morning when he saw two fishermen in the distance, cleaning their nets. When he came closer he saw they were Simon and Andrew, his first two disciples, who still carried on their trade as fishermen whenever they could. He looked down at their empty baskets.

"Simon," he said, "Row over there, where the water is deep. That is where you will find the fish!"

"Oh, Master," Simon replied, "We've

had our nets out the whole night, and we've caught nothing. Still, if you think it's worth it, we will try over there."

He pushed his boat into the lake and his brother Andrew rowed out after him in the other. They hung the net between the boats, where the water lay deep. They waited, and a stillness spread over the lake. Suddenly Simon shouted for joy. From the shore Jesus could see the two men hauling in the net, weighed down with fish that jumped and flickered in the dawn light. They filled their boats with fish and rowed back. Simon was so excited that he jumped into the water and waded ashore. He threw himself down at Jesus' feet, exclaiming, "Leave me, Lord; I am not worthy of you."

"Come with me," Jesus said to him. "From now on you will both be fishers of men."

Simon and Andrew had two friends, James and John, the sons of Zebedee, who were fishing farther down the lake. Jesus called to them too, and they left their boats and their father, and followed him.

Then Jesus went down to the harbour. He saw a tax collector named Matthew sitting at the door of his customs house. Matthew looked up and Jesus said, "Follow me!"

The people were horrified. A tax collector ought not to be a disciple of Jesus. Why, everyone knew that they were thieves and swindlers. People like the Pharisees prided themselves on never having anything to do with them. Jesus heard the people grumbling, and he said:

"I have not come to heal the healthy, but the sick. I have not come to save people who do well, but to show them how they can do better."

Then he went up into the hill country. He chose twelve men from among all his disciples, to be his apostles, and spread his teaching. They were Peter and his brother Andrew, James and John, the sons of Zebedee, Philip, Bartholomew, Thomas, Matthew, another man called James, the son of Alphaeus, Thaddaeus (who is sometimes known as Jude), Simon the Zealot, and Judas Iscariot.

Jesus sent his disciples out, two by two, in different directions. He laid his hands on them, to bless them and give them his power.

"Take nothing with you, not even money or a spare pair of sandals," he said. "When you enter a village, greet the people there and say '*Shalom*', 'Peace be with you'. If they welcome you, speak to them. Heal their sick, eat their bread. If they don't want to hear you, leave them. Don't be afraid; God will be with you. He will tell you what to say. Remember the harvest is ripe; keep praying that others will come to help you reap it."

The Sermon on the Mount

JESUS went into the hills and said to the men and women who gathered around to listen to him:

"How blessed are people who can be humble, for the Kingdom of God will be theirs.

"How blessed are people who are sad, for they will find comfort.

"How blessed are those people who have no possessions, for they will possess the whole world.

"How blessed are those who long to see goodness triumph, for they will have their wish.

"How blessed are people who show mercy to their enemies, for they will receive mercy in their turn.

"How blessed are those whose hearts are pure, for they will see God.

"How blessed are the people who are peacemakers, for God will call them his children.

"How blessed are those who suffer for the cause they know to be good, for the Kingdom of God will be theirs.

"How blessed you are when men curse you and punish you because of your love for me. Accept their insults gladly, for your reward will be great later on."

"You are like salt, without which food has no taste. You are the light for the whole world, so don't hide your light away where no one can see it. When men see what good things you are doing, they will praise God, in whose service you are doing them.

"Don't save up treasure on earth, where moths and rust will eat it away and where thieves can break in and steal it; save up treasure for yourselves in heaven where it cannot spoil and will never be stolen. For your heart will always be where the things you value are.

"Don't judge other people or they will judge you. It is easy to see the speck of dust in your friend's eye, but not so easy to admit that you have a big splinter in your own.

"First, you must take out the splinter in your own eye, then perhaps you will be able to see clearly enough to remove the dust from someone else's.

"You have heard men say, 'An eye for an eye and a tooth for a tooth.' But I say to you, it is no good fighting evil with evil. If a man hits your face on one side, offer him the other side too.

"You have heard men say, 'Love your neighbour and hate your enemy.' But I say to you, love your enemy and pray for those who hate you. Always treat other people as you would like them to treat you.

"When you pray, speak to God simply, for he knows what you need even before you ask him.

"Ask and you will get what you ask for; look and you will find what you are looking for; knock and the door will be opened.

"Every man who hears my words and follows them is like the wise man who built his house on rock. The rain fell and the floods came; the winds blew but the house did not fall down because it was built on rock. But every man who hears my words and does not follow them is like the foolish man who built his house on sand. The rain fell and the floods came; the winds blew and the house fell down because it had no foundations to hold it steady."

Jesus Calms the Storm

Jesus went on preaching to the crowds who were still gathered around him on the mountain. He said:

"No man can serve two masters; either he will hate the one and love the other, or be loyal to one and betray the other. You cannot serve both God and Money.

"So I tell you not to worry about what you should eat or what you should drink, nor what kind of clothes you should wear. Life is more important than the food that you eat, and the body is more important than the clothes that cover it.

"Look up at the birds flying in the sky. They don't sow crops nor reap them nor stow them away in barns—and yet your heavenly Father feeds them. Surely you are worth more than they are!

"Is there one of you who can make himself any taller, however hard he concentrates on worrying about it?

"So why worry about clothes? Look at the lilies growing in the field. They don't do any work and yet I tell you that Solomon in all his glory was not as splendid as they are. Now if that is how God clothes the grass in

the field which is growing today and is withered tomorrow, surely he will take even more pains to clothe you. How little faith you have in him!

"So, don't waste your time worrying about your daily needs; leave that for men who have no God to serve. God knows your needs. Concentrate on winning and deserving his love, then everything else will follow.

"Don't worry about tomorrow, for tomorrow will take care of itself."

It had grown late and night was falling. Jesus had been speaking for many hours. When he stopped at last, the crowds still sat there, waiting. He said to his disciples:

"We must cross to the other side of the lake."

So they left all the people behind and set sail across the water.

The sky grew black with clouds, and a sudden squall whipped up the waves and smashed them into the boat. The men were terrified, expecting any moment now to be spilled into the water.

"Where is Jesus?" a voice screamed into the storm. "We shall all die!" The rain lashed down as they scrambled about the boat looking for him. They found him, asleep in the stern. They pulled at his cloak to wake him.

"Rabbi! Master! Don't you care that we are drowning?" He opened his eyes and stood up. "Why are you afraid?" he asked. "Where is your faith?"

Then he called to the storm:

"Peace! Be still!"

The storm died away and the waves sank back into calm. Gradually, the stars appeared through the clouds until the night sky stretched clear and still over the earth. A sense of wonder filled all the men in the boat.

"Who can he be?" they whispered to one another. "Even the storm obeys him!"

[227]

Jesus Heals a Madman

ONE day Jesus met a madman. The man was well known in the district; he lived in graveyards and used to shout and scream all night because his mind was in such agony. People had tried to tie him down with chains, but the maniac always broke loose from them and ran off into the hills.

This man saw Jesus coming across the lake in a boat and he ran down to the shore to meet him. He cried:

"What do you want from me, Jesus, son of the most high God? For his sake, don't hurt me!"

Jesus asked him gently, "What is your name?"

"My name is Million, because we are so many," replied the evil spirits that had taken over the poor man's mind.

"Come out of him!" Jesus called to the spirits. "Go into those pigs grazing on the hill instead!"

The evil spirits obeyed him. They took possession of the pigs, so that they in turn went mad. Snorting wildly they stampeded over the edge of the hill and fell to their deaths in the lake below.

The swineherd ran away, terrified, and told the story to everyone he met. People hurried to see what was happening. There he was—the madman whose mind had been possessed by the evil spirits—sitting beside Jesus, properly dressed and perfectly sane.

The people were frightened of Jesus' power, and begged him to leave their district. So he went back to the other side of the lake.

[228]

Jairus's Daughter

As the boat drew in a man called Jairus came running down to the shore. "It's my little daughter," he sobbed. "She's very ill. She's only twelve, and she is dying. Please come and lay your hands on her so that she will live!"

Jesus went with him, followed, as always, by a crowd. A woman who had heard that Jesus could heal managed to push her way close to him. She had been ill for twelve years, and had visited many doctors; but instead of curing her they had made her worse.

"If I can only touch his clothes," she thought, "I shall be cured."

She pushed forward and brushed against his robe. At once her sickness had gone.

Jesus stopped. "Who touched me?" he asked. "I felt power flow from me."

"I did, Lord," the woman said, "Forgive me!"

"Your faith has healed you," replied Jesus. "Go in peace."

A man pushed his way up to Jairus. "It is too late!" he cried. "Your child is dead!"

"Oh, no," replied Jesus quietly. "She is not dead, she is asleep. Only believe, and she will be cured."

Then he went into the house and sent away the women who had come to weep and mourn for the child. He went into the room where the little girl lay on her bed.

"Get up, my child!" he said, and took her hand in his. She opened her eyes and stood up. Jesus smiled at her. Then he said, "Bring her some food," and left the house.

[229]

The Death of John the Baptist

JOHN the Baptist was in prison. For a long time now he had been saying things that outraged the king, Herod Antipas. No one likes to be told that he is weak and greedy, that he is no good at his job. But Herod was all these things. In his greed he had even married his brother's wife, Herodias, and taken her daughter Salome to live with them in the palace.

Herodias had been brought up in Rome and was used to luxury. Like the Romans, she liked to spend money—other people's money—on spectacular displays of dancing and acrobatics. One year she and Herod took the court to live for a time in a fort by the Dead Sea.

They had not been there long before John the Baptist demanded to speak to the king. The queen was against letting him in; she was afraid of this outspoken preacher. But Herod was curious; he had heard that John was rousing the people against him. He wanted to see this wild man from the desert for himself. "If he is dangerous," he reassured Herodias, "I will put him in prison."

John came before the king barefooted and wearing his rough camel-hair shirt.

"You are evil!" he cried. "You stole your brother's wife! You rule badly and you demand money from the poor. God's kingdom is near! God will punish you!"

The king had John arrested. He was put in prison and left there for months while Herod Antipas made up his mind what to do with him. He did not kill him for fear that John's followers would rouse the people to rebellion.

While John waited in the darkness of his prison he sent a message to Jesus. "Are you really the Messiah," he asked, "or should we expect another?"

"Tell John," Jesus replied, "that I have given sight to the blind and made the lame walk. The lepers are healed and the deaf can hear. The dead are brought back to life and the poor are hearing the good news about God. Happy is the man who does not lose his faith in me."

Then John, too, waited, with peace in his heart.

One day the king gave a party. Every high official, commander, and noble was invited. Soon everyone was drunk with wine and music.

"Where's Salome?" the king cried. "I want her to dance for us!" So she danced, and the king went wild with excitement.

"I'll give you anything you like!" he shouted, "Just ask for it!"

The girl ran off to find her mother.

"What shall I ask for?" she whispered. "Ask for the head of John the Baptist," replied the queen.

When the king heard Salome's request he was dismayed. But because he was a weak man he had to pretend to the world that he was extra strong.

"Off with his head!" he cried.

So John the Baptist died, and his head was brought to Salome on a platter.

The Parables

Every day great crowds of people gathered around Jesus to hear him speak. So that they could hear and see him better, he sometimes sat in a boat on the lake and spoke to the people on shore.

He was always telling stories, little stories, some so short that they only lasted a minute. We call them *parables*. They were about everyday things and everyday people. Within each story lay a secret meaning, which the people listening to it had to guess. These are some of the stories Jesus told.

✠

Who is like the woman who has ten silver coins and who loses one of them? She takes her lamp and looks for it everywhere; she sweeps in all the dark, forgotten corners until she finds it. And when she finds it, she calls her friends together to tell them the good news. God is like this; when we leave him and do wrong, he looks for us everywhere, and when he finds us again he is glad.

✠

What is like a mustard seed? Remember, it is one of the smallest of all seeds, and yet when it is sown in the ground, it grows bigger than all the other plants in the garden, and has great branches for the birds to nest in? The answer is the Kingdom of God. You cannot see it, but the seed of it is already sown, in the hearts of men. One day it will shoot up and grow great.

A man once went out to sow grain in his fields. Some of the seed fell on a path, and the birds came and pecked it up. Some of the seed fell on stony ground where there was hardly any earth. It sprouted up at once, but when the sun rose it was parched by the heat and withered away because the earth there was not deep enough to water its roots. Some of the seed fell among thorn bushes, and the bushes shot up and choked it. But some of the seed fell on good earth, and when it grew ripe it bore fine full ears of wheat, and the man harvested sixty times what he had sown.

Who is like the man who owns 100 sheep and loses one of them? He leaves the 99 of them on the hillside while he goes into the valley to look for the one that is lost. And when he has found it he slings it over his shoulders, and joyfully brings it back. Then he calls his friends and neighbours together. "Come and celebrate with me," he says to them, "for I have found the sheep that I had lost."

God is like this shepherd. There is more joy in heaven over one man who has lived badly and then is sorry and becomes good than over 99 people who were on the right road all the time.

✠

The Kingdom of Heaven is like buried treasure which is lying hidden in a field. A man comes across it accidentally – then he buries it again, and goes off overjoyed to sell all his possessions to buy that field.

Or think of the Kingdom of Heaven as being like a pearl of great value; a man will go and sell everything he has to buy it.

OUR Father in Heaven may be compared to a master who went out before sunrise to hire men to work in his vineyard.

He hired them for the whole day, and it was arranged they they should each earn one piece of silver. They began work soon after sunrise.

Now the grape harvest was so great that the master needed still more labourers. Three hours later he again went out and hired more men. "Join the others in the vineyard," he said. "I will give you a fair wage."

At midday he was still short of hands, so he went out and hired some more. He did the same again in the afternoon.

Eleven hours after the first man had begun to work, he went out again and saw some men standing about.

"Why aren't you working?" he asked.

"Because no one has hired us," they replied, and the master said to them:

"Go to my vineyard and pick the grapes."

When darkness fell, the master called all the men together and gave them each one silver piece, regardless of how long they had worked. What was more, he paid the men he had taken on last before he paid the ones he had taken on first.

Some of the labourers began grumbling. They said, "These fellows here have only put in one hour's work, and you've treated them exactly the same as us—yet we've had to go through all the hard work and the heat of the day!"

But he replied, "My friends, I am not being unfair to you. We agreed on a wage of one piece of silver a day? So take your money and go home. I happen to want to give the late comers as much as I give you. Must you be jealous because I am generous?"

God's love is like that. It falls on all of us alike.

✠

THERE was once a man who had two sons. The younger one said to his father:

"Father, give me my share of the farm and the lands that will come to me one day."

So the man divided up his property between the two sons. Soon afterwards, the younger son collected his belongings and went off to see the world. He lived carelessly and spent freely. Soon he had no money left at all. Then a terrible famine arose in that country, and he began to go hungry. He went to work for a man who sent him out into the fields to feed the pigs. He grew so hungry that he would have eaten even the pig swill in the trough, but no one gave him anything.

One day he came to his senses and said to himself: "Why, my father's servants have more food than they can eat, and here am I, dying of hunger! I will get up and go back to my father, and I will say to him, 'Father, I have done wrong in the sight of heaven and in your eyes. I don't deserve to be called your son. Please take me on as one of your servants.'"

So he left his master and went back home. But while he was still some distance away his father saw him coming and felt a surge of love for him. He ran out to meet him and hugged and kissed him. Then the son tried to pull away.

"Father," he said, "I have done wrong in the sight of heaven and in your eyes. I don't deserve to be called your son any more—"

But his father still held him close. "Hurry!" he called to his servants, "Fetch the best clothes in the house and put them on my son. Put a ring on his finger and shoes on his feet, and get the calf we've been fattening and kill it, so that we can have a feast and celebrate! My son has come home! I thought he was dead, and he is alive—I thought I had lost him, and he is found!"

✠

ONE year a farmer had a very good harvest. He said to himself, "How rich I am! I must build bigger barns, to store it all! Now I can relax; I've got enough food for years to come. I'm the luckiest soul on earth; I've got everything I want!"

But God said to him, "You fool, this very night you will die, and your soul will be taken from you. You have been so greedy in collecting food for your body that you have starved your soul to death!"

✠

WHAT is like the yeast which a housewife mixes with flour and water into a dough, and leaves in a bowl to rise? The answer is the Kingdom of God, because it will rise and fill the earth just as surely as the yeast sponge rises and fills the bowl.

ISRAEL is like a vineyard which was much loved by its owner. He took great care of it, and had fenced it round and built a watch-tower on it. Then he let the vineyard to some farmers and went abroad. At the end of the season he sent a servant to collect his share of the harvest. But the tenants beat the servant and sent him back empty-handed.

The owner sent another servant, and another, but each time the same thing happened. In the end he sent his son, saying to himself, "They will surely respect my son."

But they didn't. When the son came to his father's house, he knocked on the door, and the tenants opened it and killed him. Then the owner came himself, destroyed those evil men, and gave his vineyard to new tenants.

✠

"GOD says that we must love our neighbour as much as we love ourselves," said a scholar one day to Jesus, "But who exactly *is* my neighbour?"

Jesus replied:

"There was once a man who was travelling from Jerusalem to Jericho. He was attacked by bandits who beat him up, stripped off his clothes, and left him by the roadside, half dead.

"A priest came by soon afterwards and saw the man lying there, but he did not stop. Instead he walked past, keeping on the other side of the road. Then a Temple official came by. He, too, saw the man, but he looked the other way and went on.

"Then a Samaritan, a stranger in those parts, came along the road. As soon as he saw the man he felt sorry for him. He went up to him, cleaned his wounds with oil and wine, and bandaged them. Then he lifted the man onto his own mule, and took him to an inn, and looked after him there. The next day he gave the innkeeper two pieces of silver and said, 'Look after him for me. If you have to spend any more than this, I will repay you when I pass here on my return.'"

"Which of these men," asked Jesus, "was a good neighbour?"

"Without any doubt, the one who gave help," replied the scholar.

✠

GOOD and evil grow side by side in this world, like wheat and weeds. But when the time comes God will separate the one from the other.

He will burn the evil in the world as a farmer burns his weeds in a bonfire, and keep the good, as the wheat is harvested and kept carefully in a barn.

ONCE upon a time a wealthy man made plans to go abroad for a while, on business. He did not want to take his money with him, and he did not want to lock it away. So he distributed it among his servants and asked them to look after it for him.

One servant received five bags of money, another received two, and a third got just one. Each man received as much as he could manage. Then the master went on his trip.

The man who had received the five bags went off and traded with them. He worked so well that in the end he had doubled the amount of his master's money.

The man to whom the master had given two bags also earned another two.

But the third man, who had been given only one bag, went off and buried it in the ground and hid it, because he was afraid of losing it.

When the master came back and saw how hard the first two servants had worked for him, he was glad, and rewarded them. But when he saw the third man return his bag of money exactly as it was when he gave it to him, he was angry. "You should have had more courage!" he said. "You should have used your chance to do better. If you do something worthwhile with your life it will grow richer, but if you do nothing you will be left with nothing."

✠

THERE was once a rich man called Dives. A poor man used to live in the street outside his house and beg for food. The poor man's name was Lazarus. Both men fell ill and died. Lazarus was carried straight to heaven because he had suffered so much during his life, but Dives had to stay outside. He had not helped Lazarus while he was alive; he had left him in all his misery outside his house gate. Now God left Dives outside the gate of heaven because it was his turn to suffer.

ONCE upon a time there was a judge who neither feared God nor respected his fellow men. There was a widow in the town who kept coming to him and saying, "Please protect me from this man who is trying to ruin me." For a long time the judge refused to do anything about it. But one day he said to himself, "It would really be much simpler to give this woman what she wants, and be able to live in peace." If a man who does not like his fellow creatures is willing to help those who ask him, surely God will do much more for you when you ask him for help, because he loves you!

✠

THE Kingdom of Heaven is like a wedding feast. There are ten bridesmaids, all waiting to meet the bridegroom. Five of them are thoughtless, five of them are sensible. The thoughtless ones take lamps to meet the bridegroom, but they forget to put any oil inside them. The sensible ones fill their lamps up first and then go out to wait for the bridegroom to arrive.

The bridegroom and his friends are a long time coming, and the ten girls grow very weary. Finally, they all fall asleep.

Then, in the middle of the night comes the cry, "Here is the bridegroom!
Go out and meet him!"

The girls get up quickly and trim their lamps to make them give a good light.

"Our lamps are going out!" the thoughtless girls say to the others. "Let us have some of your oil to fill them up." "Oh no!" the sensible ones answer, "There isn't enough oil for all of us. We must greet the Master with lighted lamps! You can't borrow light from someone else's lamp; each of us must carry her own."

The silly girls hurry off to look for oil, and while they are gone the bridegroom comes. The sensible girls join in the wedding procession and are welcomed to the feast. But by the time the thoughtless girls have found some oil and hurried back, they are too late; the doors are shut when they return, and they cannot go in and join in the feast.

Our Father in Heaven may be compared to a king who decided to make his servants pay him back all the money they owed him. A man was brought to him who owed a million bags of gold. When the king saw that his servant could not possibly repay the debt, he gave orders that the man should be sold as a slave, along with his wife and children and all his possessions. The servant fell on his knees in front of the king and begged him for mercy.

"Just give me time and I will pay you back every penny!" he cried. The king was sorry for him, so he let him go and released him from the whole of the debt.

But when this same servant was free again, he found one of his fellow servants who owed him a few pieces of silver. He grabbed him by the throat and cried:

"Pay up what you owe me!"

The other man fell down at his feet and begged him for time to pay back the debt. But the servant would not listen. He had the man sent to prison. The king heard about his cruel behaviour and sent for him.

"You wicked servant!" he exclaimed, "I let you off the whole of your debt because I was sorry for you. Why didn't you treat your debtor with the same kindness that I had shown to you?"

He wasted no more words; he had the servant thrown into prison, to remain there until he had repaid his debt.

✠

ONCE upon a time a man planned a big feast and invited a great many people. He sent his servants out to tell them, "Come today, everything is ready." But they all made excuses. One man said to him, "I have bought some land; I must go and look at it; I can't come today." Another man said, "I have bought some oxen and have to try them out today. Please excuse me." A third man said, "I have just got married; I am sure you will understand that I am rather busy and can't come today."

When the master heard all these excuses he was angry. He said to his servant, "Hurry out into the streets and alleys of the town and bring in the poor people and all the sick people who are crippled, blind or lame. Then, when you have done this, go out to the country roads and invite all the poor and homeless people to come and eat and drink with me."

It is the same with God; the people who have no time for his Kingdom now, will never see it, but those who come will have plenty of everything.

✠

JESUS said: "I am the Good Shepherd. A good shepherd will give his life for the sake of his sheep. A man who does not own the sheep, who is only hired to look after them, will think first of his own safety. When he sees a wolf coming he will run away and leave the sheep unprotected. But the good shepherd knows each of his sheep by name. He lets them out of the fold, and when he has gathered them around him he leads them to the pastures, and they follow him because they know his voice and they are safe.

"I am the Good Shepherd; I know that the sheep are mine and they know that I protect them, just as the Father knows me and I know the Father. I will give my life to save my sheep.

"And I have other sheep, too, who belong to other folds. But I will lead them as well, and they will listen to my voice. I will gather them all together, and there will be one flock and one shepherd."

Jesus and the Children

MOTHERS used to bring their children to Jesus so that he should bless them. They were simple, good women who did not understand the words that educated people spoke to Jesus. But in their hearts they knew what was most important about him: that he brought with him the love of God and that this would make their children strong.

When the disciples saw the children standing shyly around Jesus they grew angry.

"Come, come," they said to the mothers, "you're wasting his time. He's got more important people to talk to than children!"

"No one is more important than these children," said Jesus. He made the children come close to him and then he said to the men standing by:

"If you are so proud and so filled with your own importance you will never be able to see the Kingdom of God. You must feel as small as these children, and as powerless, before you can see God.

"Take care never to hurt a child, for my Father who is in heaven has sent his angels to watch over them."

Then he said to them, "Don't imagine that you are better than other men, nor even better than these children. Don't be proud, like the man in this story:

"Two men went up to the Temple to pray. One was a Pharisee, a learned man, the other was a tax collector whom everyone despised because of his work. While the Pharisee was taking off his shoes before entering the Temple he saw the tax collector coming through the courtyard. The Pharisee walked quickly on, past a crowd of people whom he despised—Romans, women, slaves, cripples

–who were not allowed into the inner courtyard of the Temple. When he reached the
main steps he stood in front of the great
doors that lead to the altar.

"'Oh God,' he prayed, flinging up his
arms and raising his voice so that it would
carry all round the courtyard, 'I thank you
that I am not like the common people whom
I saw outside this Temple. I am glad that I
am not greedy, dishonest, impure. I am even
more glad that I'm not like that miserable
tax collector over there. I fast twice a week,
I give a tenth part of my earnings to charity;
I do everything the Scriptures say I should.'

"The tax collector, meanwhile, had stayed
in a distant corner of the courtyard. He did
not even raise his eyes. He moved his hands
in a gesture of despair and folded them over
his chest. Then he prayed quietly: 'I have
sinned and done wrong–please, God, forgive me.'

"Which of these two men was closer to
God?" asked Jesus. "Which one was loved
by God, and forgiven?"

The Feeding of the Five Thousand

Jesus said to his disciples, "Come, let us go to a quiet place to rest." He set off with them by boat, but the people did not want him to go, and a great crowd followed him along the shore.

They seemed to be so lost, like sheep without a shepherd, that Jesus was filled with pity for them. He steered his boat back to the shore and spoke to them about God, and healed everyone who was sick.

Evening came, and the disciples said, "This is a lonely place and it's getting late. Send the people away, Lord, while it's still light, so that they can find themselves something to eat."

He answered, "Let them have our food. How much do we need to fill them all?"

Philip answered, "We need at least 200 pieces of silver to buy enough bread to fill all these people. There must be close on 5,000 of them. And there's no bread to buy."

"How much food have we got?" Jesus asked. Andrew came up with a small boy. "This little fellow's got five barley loaves and two fish," he said. "He says we can have them if we like. But that won't be enough to feed 5,000 people!"

Jesus said, "Tell everyone to sit down. Arrange them in small groups to make it easier to pass the food around."

Then he took the five loaves and two fish and looked up to heaven. He gave God thanks for the food, and broke the bread into pieces. Then he divided the fish, and gave all the pieces to the disciples and the small boy to distribute.

Everyone of the 5,000 people ate and no one went hungry. When they had all had enough Jesus said:

"Collect the food that is left over, so that nothing is wasted."

"Not everyone who calls me, 'Lord, Lord,' will enter the Kingdom of Heaven. Only the man who does what my Father wants him to do during his life will enter it in the end. Just *talking* about God is not enough; *doing* what he says is more important."

They picked up the remaining food and filled twelve baskets with the scraps.

Then Jesus went up into the hills and taught his disciples alone. "I am the bread of life," he told them. "Anyone who comes to me will not be hungry, and the man who believes in me will never be thirsty.

As they came back Jesus saw a blind man sitting by the road. "Why is that man blind?" his disciples asked. "Is God punishing him, or his parents, because they did wrong?" Jesus replied, "Men do not suffer like that because they have done wrong, but to show the power of God working in them. Now I bring light to the blind, for I am the light of the world." And he made the man see again.

"When you pray, say to God quietly: 'Our Father in Heaven, holy is your name; may your Kingdom come, may your will be done on earth as it is in heaven. Give us enough bread for this day. Forgive us the wrong we have done, as we have forgiven those who have wronged us. Keep us from being tempted to do what we should not do, and save us from evil.'

Jesus Walks on the Water

"GO HOME now," said Jesus to the people who had gathered around him. "Sleep well tonight, and tomorrow morning wake up and praise God. Live each day gladly, and without fear."

The people left. Jesus turned to his disciples. "Leave me too, for I have to pray. I must be alone, to receive strength from God. Today I gave each man and woman and child whom I healed a portion of my strength. Just as a well can be drained of its water, so the water of life has drained from within me. I must go up into the mountains now, so that the heavenly Father can fill me with his strength again in the stillness of night."

The disciples were sad, because they would have preferred to spend the night with their master. But they pushed the keel of their boat down from the beach and pulled up the anchor. They waded into the shallow water and pulled the boat after them. When it had gone out far enough to carry their weight they climbed in and hoisted sail.

Their headway was slow. The lights from the farmhouses on the other side of the lake grew no bigger, the hills behind the houses no nearer. The boat was sailing almost directly into the wind, and it seemed to stand still. The lights on the shore went out and the darkness around them was complete.

The disciples grew afraid. Once again there was nothing to steer by, only the wind driving hard into their faces as if it were trying to push them back.

Suddenly, they caught sight of a figure moving towards them over the water. Then they recognized it – it was Jesus, walking on the waves, the wind blowing his cloak out behind him. A light shone from him and they were terrified.

"It's a ghost!" they cried.

"It is I," replied Jesus. "Don't be afraid."

Simon Peter, who was always the first to speak and to act, said:

"Lord, if it really is you, let me come to you over the water."

"Come, then," called Jesus.

Peter stepped down from the boat. He walked on the water, and it held him up. He had come quite close to Jesus when a gust of wind blew spray into his face and made the water foam around him. Then he looked down and was terrified.

"Help me, Lord!" he cried, as the water covered his feet. But the more afraid he grew, the faster he sank. At once Jesus stretched out his arms and held him up.

"You only sank because you were afraid, Peter," he said. "Where was your faith in me?"

The wind dropped and they returned to the boat and climbed in. Then the whole crew kneeled down around Jesus. "You are really the Son of God!" they told him.

Jesus Foretells the Crucifixion

JESUS took his disciples to the hill country of Caesarea Philippi where the source of the river Jordan was.

There he turned to them and said, "What do people say about me? Who do they say I am?"

"Well," they replied, "some say you are John the Baptist. Some say Elijah or maybe Jeremiah or some other prophet."

"And you—who do you say I am?"

"I say you are the Messiah, the Son of the living God!" replied Peter. Jesus said:

"You are blessed, Simon son of John, for my Father who is in Heaven has revealed this to you! You are Peter the Rock, and on your rock I will build my Church. It will be stronger than all the power of darkness."

Then Jesus began to prepare his disciples for the time of sorrow that lay ahead. He told them how he would have to go to Jerusalem, how the leaders there would make him suffer and how he would be put to death.

"God forbid, Lord! This must never happen!" exclaimed Peter in dismay.

Jesus spoke to him sharply. "Go away and don't tempt me as the Devil did, Peter!

You think only of what you want, not of what God wants."

Then he said, "If any man wants to follow me he must give up everything and carry a cross. For whoever tries to save himself will lose his life, and whoever loses his life for my sake will save it."

Jesus took Simon Peter, James and his brother John into the mountains with him.

As they climbed higher the air grew cooler and lighter, and the country stretched out beneath them. It was evening. Jesus looked down onto the Promised Land, the land of Israel. Its ridges and valleys lay sharp and beautiful under the setting sun.

Then darkness closed in on them. It was night. They were high above the world, high above the homes of men.

Peter, James and John leaned back in the shelter of a boulder; they were very tired. Jesus prayed to God. Suddenly his whole appearance changed; his face shone with the glory of God, and his clothes were so brilliantly white that they blazed with light. Moses and Elijah stood beside him, talking to him.

"Oh, Master!" Peter cried out. "It is wonderful to be here. If you like, I could put up three tabernacles, one for you, one for Moses, and one for Elijah."

He was so excited and afraid that he hardly knew what he was saying. While he was talking a bright cloud of light came down over the mountain and covered them, so that they could see nothing. A voice said out of the cloud:

"This is my beloved Son. Listen to him."

The three disciples fell to the ground, hiding their faces. At last they looked up. Jesus was standing alone, a little way off. There was a sense of stillness and peace in the air. Jesus came back to them and touched them gently.

"Stand up," he said. "Don't be afraid. But don't tell anyone about this yet."

The Journey to Jerusalem

JESUS was on the road to Jerusalem when a young man came up to him. He was the son of rich parents and admired Jesus greatly. "Master, tell me please," he asked, "what must I do to be sure of eternal life?"

"You must follow God's commandments," Jesus replied.

"Master," replied the man, "I have obeyed all these ever since I was a child."

Jesus looked at him. "Then there is one thing you still must do. Go and sell everything you have and give the money to the poor, for God will give you riches in heaven. Then come back and follow me."

When the young man heard this he was startled and disturbed. He had many beautiful possessions and he just could not bear to live without them. Jesus watched him going sadly away, then he said to his disciples, "It is actually easier for a camel to go through the eye of a needle than for a rich man to enter the Kingdom of God."

Jesus and his disciples went on their way to Jerusalem. As they came to one village, ten lepers came limping towards Jesus.

"Save us, Master!" they cried to him.

Jesus healed them, and the lepers hurried off. Only one among them, a stranger to the district, turned back and came to kneel at Jesus' feet. "Thank you, Lord, for healing me," he said, looking up at him.

"Your faith has cured you," Jesus answered, "for you have remembered to thank God."

Jesus Visits the Home of Mary and Martha

ON HIS way to Jerusalem Jesus stopped in the village of Bethany at the home of two sisters, Martha and Mary.

"Jesus has come to see us!" Martha called to her sister. She felt very important. "Quick! Get to work! We must show him what we can do. We'll give him a better meal than he'd have anywhere else. We don't want anyone to say we are poor or mean!"

She was in such a hurry that she hardly found time to greet Jesus properly as he entered. Mary fell on her knees, saying:

"Welcome, Lord. You bring joy and peace to us!" She led him through to the courtyard and he sat down. Then she sat down beside him, and he began to speak of God and of our need to empty our hearts of all things except his love. As Mary looked into Jesus' face and listened to his voice, a great calm came over her.

"What he says is more important than anything else in the world," she thought. "I must stay here with him, not go to the kitchen. I must live for this moment, not for later, when he is gone. God has given me this moment to enjoy."

Martha came out of the kitchen. Her face was red from the heat and the hurry, and her

hands were wet with the fish she had cleaned. She was angry with her sister.

"Lord, won't you tell Mary to help me with the cooking?" she asked Jesus. "There's so much to do!"

"Martha, Martha," Jesus replied. "You worry too much about small things. Do one thing at a time, and only the most important. Mary knows what that is."

The two sisters looked at him. Had he not said once that his words were more than food and wine?

Later, Jesus said to his disciples:

"The Son of Man has come to give his life so that others may be set free."

Jesus often called himself the Son of Man. It was what the prophet Daniel had called the Messiah, the Saviour who would come one day to lead the people back to the Kingdom of God. The Son of Man was the secret name for Christ.

"You must not be sad," Jesus went on. "You must hold fast to your faith in God and your faith in me. The place where my Father will lead you when everything is over is large, like a house with many rooms. I am going there now, to get a place ready for you. One day I will come back to lead you there.

"Now you know where I am going and the road I will take to get there."

"But, Master," said Thomas, "that's just it. We don't know where you are going. So how can we know the way there?"

"I am the way, I am the truth and I am life," Jesus replied. "All you need to do is to follow me."

Lazarus Is Brought Back to Life

ONE day Lazarus fell ill. He grew steadily worse, and Martha and Mary sent a message to Jesus:

"Come quickly, Lord, and heal our brother!"

But Jesus' followers were frightened. "Don't go back to Bethany!" they begged. "Not long ago the people there tried to stone you."

"I must," replied Jesus. "Lazarus has already fallen asleep and I must wake him."

When they reached Bethany they found that Lazarus had died, and, as was the custom in hot countries, they had buried his body at once.

"Oh, Lord," Martha sobbed, "if only you had come sooner, you could have saved him!"

"Your brother will rise again," Jesus replied.

"Yes, I know that," said Martha, "When the day of resurrection comes–"

"I am the resurrection and I am life," Jesus told her. "If a man believes in me he will never die. Do you realize that?"

"Yes, Lord, I do," said Martha, "I believe you are Christ, the Son of God."

"Take me to his grave," said Jesus.

The grave was in a cave, and they had to roll a stone away from the entrance to open it. The people murmured, "Why didn't he save his friend Lazarus?"

Jesus wept. He wept because they did not understand that with God there is no death.

"Lazarus, come out!" he cried.

Shuffling, because his hands and feet were still bound in the winding sheet of the dead, Lazarus came out. The crowd of people gasped in amazement; all Jesus said was:

"Unbind him and let him go home."

Jesus' Enemies Plot to Kill Him

THE Pharisees were keeping a careful eye on Jesus. There were several reasons why they wanted him out of the way. They met in council with the chief priests of Jerusalem to discuss what they should do. A priest rose and said:

"This Jesus is dangerous. He can perform miracles, there's no doubt about it. But if we let him go on like this his power over people will grow enormous. They'll follow him everywhere. They'll do whatever he tells them!"

"Yes," said another official, "And then what would happen? The Romans wouldn't like it. They'd think we were getting too independent. They'd be afraid we would want to break away from the Empire. We wouldn't be allowed any more public meetings, or Temple worship."

"What can we do? Send him away? Put him in prison? He's too popular, besides, he's done nothing wrong."

Then Caiaphas the high priest of the Temple, rose.

"Jesus must die," he said. "It's in our own interest. It's better for one man to die than that the whole nation should be destroyed."

The Pharisees went to the Roman governor in Jerusalem.

"Look," they said, "We don't want Jesus around any more than you do. We wouldn't mind in the least if you had him killed. We will lure him into saying something against you, and then you can charge him with treason."

They sent some young men to question Jesus. A few of Herod's men went with them as witnesses.

"Master," one of the young rabbis asked innocently, "Do you think it's right to pay taxes to Caesar? I mean, ought we, the Jews, to pay taxes to a foreign king?"

But Jesus realized that the question was a trap. "Bring me a coin," he replied, "and I will tell you."

The coin was brought. Jesus held it up. "Whose head is stamped on this?" he asked.

"Caesar's," they replied.

"Then give to Caesar the things that are Caesar's, and to God the things that are God's. Pay Caesar his taxes. That is not what matters. The point is, who do you really worship? God? Caesar? Money?"

They were so astonished at his words that they had nothing more to say. After this, Jesus stopped going about Jerusalem openly and taught his disciples in a remote town in the hill country.

But his enemies continued to plot. They met once again at the high priest's palace. There were several men present who respected Jesus, and did not want him harmed. But they kept silent because they were afraid that they would be expelled from the synagogue and would lose their jobs if they spoke up for him now.

Caiaphas proposed that they should capture Jesus and hand him over to the Romans.

"Yes, but why do we really want him to die?" one man asked. Caiaphas replied:

"Because he behaves as if he were God. This is blasphemy and he must die for it."

Jesus Warns the Disciples of What Lies Ahead

JESUS prepared himself for the last stage of his journey. When people saw him going towards Jerusalem they were amazed. Everyone knew his enemies there were plotting how to kill him. But Jesus was going to Jerusalem to attend the feast of the Passover, when every Jewish household would sacrifice a lamb to God. Men believed that they would be made pure again because an innocent creature had died for them.

"The Passover will soon begin," Jesus told his disciples, "and the Son of Man will be betrayed by his own people, into the hands of the chief priests and Pharisees. Then he will be handed over to men who do not

believe in God. They will jeer at him and spit in his face. They will beat him and kill him. But after three days he will rise again."

Jesus was at Bethany having supper with Lazarus and his sisters. As they sat at table Mary brought a flask filled with a rare and precious oil. She poured it over Jesus' feet and wiped them dry with her long hair.

As the rich perfume filled the room, Judas, the disciple in charge of the money, muttered, "We could have sold that bottle and given the money to the poor."

"Let Mary be," said Jesus. "She has done a beautiful thing. She has anointed me in preparation for my death."

The Entry into Jerusalem

ON HIS way to Jerusalem Jesus passed through Jericho.

"Jesus of Nazareth is coming! They say that he's the Messiah!" The word went round from street to street.

People crowded along the roadside to see him pass. Among them was a man called Zacchaeus, who wanted to see Jesus more than anything else in the world. He tried to elbow his way to the front of the crowd, but the people pushed him back. No one liked him because he was a tax collector and had Romans as his friends. He was a little man, and he knew that he would never see Jesus from behind all those people. So he climbed up a tree to get a better view.

Jesus walked by. Hundreds of people thronged about him, touching him and being blessed by him. Suddenly he looked up and saw Zacchaeus in the tree.

"Come down, Zacchaeus," he called, "Tonight I am going to stay at your house."

The next day Jesus set out for Jerusalem. He took two of his disciples aside and said to them:

"Go into the village on the slopes of the Mount of Olives. You will find a donkey there, which no one has yet ridden. Untie it and bring it here."

They brought the donkey to him, and he mounted it. Then they climbed up along the stony road that led towards the city.

[257]

Wherever he went the people threw their cloaks down in front of him on the dusty stones, as if they were laying a carpet for a king. Children plucked leaves off the hedges and scattered them before him, and strewed flowers at his feet.

Still more people came, waving branches they had pulled from the palm trees alongside the road. They sang:

"Hosannah! The son of David! He comes in the name of the Lord! Blessed is he!"

"Don't let them say such things about you, Master!" said a Pharisee, who was shocked

that the people should be so happy. But Jesus answered:

"I tell you that if the people were silent the stones would cry out to welcome me!"

He entered the Temple, followed by a great crowd of people, singing and waving palms. The Temple guards and the scholars and lawyers were outraged.

"Stop that shouting!" they said, but no one took any notice. The priests and lawyers turned away in anger.

"He must be arrested!" they said. "He is leading the people into rebellion!"

The Withered Fig Tree

JESUS was hungry. He looked around for food, and saw a fig tree standing by the road. Its branches were strong; its leaves hung dense and green over the earth. It looked as if it would have plenty of fruit, just as Jerusalem looked as if it would be full of the people who loved God.

The midday heat rose from the stone path. Jesus walked through it to the tree. He drew the branches apart and raised his hand to pluck the fruit. But the branches were empty. The tree was a sham; it held no fruit, just as the priests and scholars of Jerusalem held no love for the Son of Man.

"Nothing will ever grow on you!" said Jesus, and at once the fig tree withered away.

Jesus stopped on the Mount of Olives and looked down onto the city, saying sadly:

"Oh, Jerusalem, Jerusalem!
  You murder the prophets
  And stone the messengers sent to you!
  How often I have wanted to gather your
    children
  As a hen gathers her chicks under her
    wings,
  But you would not let me!"

Then he turned to his disciples. "The time will come," he said, "when men will forget God, and their love will grow cold. Then they will hate you because of me."

Jesus Drives the Money Changers out of the Temple

JESUS went into the Temple. To the right and left of him squatted beggars, stretching out their hands to him. Jesus spoke to them, and gave them his blessing. In the forecourt sat the blind and the lame; they were not allowed to come any further. Jesus healed them and passed on.

He came to another courtyard. Here the smell and the noise resembled a cattle market before the Passover. Rams were straining at their chains; kids and lambs butted and trembled in their pens, while doves and pigeons beat their wings against their cages trying to fly out and escape. Most people did not bring their own animals to sacrifice, so all these creatures were waiting to be bought and killed as offerings to God.

Above the noise of the frightened beasts could be heard the shouting and swearing of the men who owned them. From time to time an animal would break loose and its owner would chase it through the crowd, roughly pushing aside the people who had come there to pray.

He, in turn, would be laughed at by the money changers who sat in long rows at their tables, with piles of coins stacked in front of them.

Jesus stood still. He must have remembered the words of the prophet Malachi: *"Suddenly the Lord will come to the Temple . . . and he will cleanse the Temple . . . ."*

He made a rough whip out of some cord that was lying on the ground. Then he raised his arm and brought the whip down on the piles of coins, so that they rolled across the yard. He scattered the cages, so that they burst open and the birds flew away. He raised his whip in the direction of the traders, and they left their goods and ran out of the Temple. He kicked down the pens, so that lambs and kids scampered into the streets. Finally he overturned the tables themselves, and scattered their benches in disorder.

"Take all this away!" he cried.

The priests and the Temple guards came rushing to see what had happened. When he saw them, Jesus cried in a voice of terrible anger:

"It is written in the Scriptures '*My house shall be a house of prayer for all people.*' But you have made it into a den of thieves!"

Jesus Answers the Sadducees and the Pharisees

THE Pharisees already disliked Jesus. Now they were joined by the Sadducees, another religious group who worshipped slightly differently from the Pharisees, and did not believe in a resurrection—the bringing back to life of everyone who had died believing in God. Together they tried to set a trap for Jesus. When they saw him coming to the Temple to teach they brought him a woman who had been unfaithful to her husband.

"The laws Moses gave us say that this woman should be stoned to death," they said. "What do you say to that?"

As if he had not heard them, Jesus bent down and began to write in the dust. They repeated their question. He stood up and looked at them.

"Let the man among you who has never done anything wrong throw the first stone at her," he said.

Then he stooped down again and went on writing on the ground.

The men were silent. Not one among them could say he had never sinned. So they went away one by one. Then Jesus said quietly to the woman:

"Go home now, and do not sin again."

The Widow's Gift

SOON after that the High Council in Jerusalem published a decree. A herald proclaimed:

"Jesus of Nazareth is leading the people astray. He is making them ignore the laws of Moses. Anyone who knows where he is must inform the High Council, so that he can be arrested, and tried."

Wherever Jesus went, he was followed by a crowd of people. They formed a protective wall around him, so that the Temple guards dared not arrest him.

One day it happened that he was teaching in the women's court in the Temple. He talked about giving. To love and to give, he said, was more important than anything else.

A widow came in; she was old and bent and obviously very poor. Nobody seemed to see her except Jesus. Another woman came in; she was young and rich and everyone noticed *her*. The gold bracelets on her arms and ankles tinkled. She threw a handful of money into the Temple offering box and the sound of the large coins dropping echoed from wall to wall. The widow held one coin hidden in her hand. It was small, and it was all that she had. Quietly she dropped it into the box.

Jesus said, "The rich give a little of what they have; they give what they don't need. This widow has given God her last coin; she trusts him and gives him everything. Her love is richer than all the money in the world, and God will reward her with great blessings and joy."

Jesus Describes the Day of Judgment

JESUS said, "At the end of time the Son of Man will return. The sun will grow dark and the moon will cease to give light, the stars will disappear and the air and sky will shake. Then the Son of Man will appear riding on the clouds in great splendour.

"He will gather everyone from every corner of the earth together, and separate them one from another as a shepherd separates the sheep from the goats. Those who have led good lives will be on his right, those who have been wicked on his left.

"He will say to those on his right, 'Come, O blessed people, it is time for you to inherit the kingdom prepared for you. When I was hungry you gave me food, when I was thirsty you gave me drink, when I was a stranger you welcomed me, when I was naked you clothed me, when I was sick you visited me, when I was in prison you came to me.' Then the good people will say, 'Lord, when did we do all those things?' and he will reply, 'When you did them to the least important person you can think of, you were doing them to me.'

"Then he will say to those on his left, 'Because you did not do these things freely to anyone, you did not do them to me. Leave me—you are cursed for ever.'"

Judas Plots Against Jesus

THE chief priests and elders were holding another meeting. They were in the palace of the high priest Caiaphas. Yet again, the subject was how to get rid of Jesus of Nazareth.

Jesus, meanwhile, was speaking to his disciples on a hill outside the city. He said:

"I have not come to judge the world, but to save it. I am the light of the world; if you follow me you will never walk in darkness, but will live all your lives in the light. You will know the truth and the truth will set you free."

One of the twelve men, Judas Iscariot, left Jesus suddenly. He ran all the way back to Jerusalem, to the palace of the high priest.

"Let me in!" he cried, knocking on the heavy door. "I have something important to say!"

He was brought before Caiaphas and his council.

"What do you want, Judas Iscariot?"

"I want to destroy Jesus," Judas replied. "Once I believed in his teaching; now I do not. I cannot stand his love. I will take you to him."

"We usually pay our spies," said Caiaphas. "How much do you want?"

Judas shrugged his shoulders. "Pay what you like," he said.

Caiaphas hated Jesus. "The usual price for a slave is 30 pieces of silver," he said. "Will you take that?"

"Yes," replied Judas, "I will."

The Last Supper

JESUS took Peter and John aside and said to them:

"It is time to prepare the Passover supper. Go into Jerusalem, to the well of Siloam. You will meet a man there, carrying a pitcher of water. Follow him, and when you reach the house he enters, say to the master of the house, 'Our Master says, My time has come. I will celebrate the Feast of the Passover in your house.'"

Peter and John did as Jesus said. They were led to an upper room, with a low table in it, set round with three benches—just enough room for thirteen people. They laid out the food prescribed for the feast: bitter herbs and nuts, raisins and figs, vinegar, salt and a jar of wine. The oil lamps were trimmed, the unleavened bread was baking in the oven. Only the lamb was missing.

When all was ready Jesus came. He brought the other apostles with him, and they climbed up the stone staircase to the upper room. Below them lay the city, its people filled with happiness as they celebrated their release from slavery in Egypt. It was their night of salvation and freedom.

Jesus went to the head of the table. He gave the blessing and passed around the bitter herbs, dipped in vinegar. Suddenly he stood up, took off his long robe and tied a towel around himself like a servant. He took a basin and a jar of water and began to wash the feet of his disciples. Peter exclaimed:

"Lord! You mustn't wash my feet!"

Jesus kneeled in front of him. "Unless you let me wash you," he replied, "You cannot share what is going to happen to me. I am making myself humble before you and you must make yourselves humble before others.

Servants and masters are equal in the eyes of God."

When he had washed their feet and dried them, he took the flat, unleavened bread in his hands. "Praise be to you, Oh God, who have made the bread come from the earth," he said. But instead of adding the usual words the Jews spoke at the blessing, "This is the bread of misery which our fathers ate . . ." he held it up and said, "This is my body, which I am giving for you." Then he broke it, and shared the pieces among them.

He poured the red wine into the big cup, and thanked God with these words, "Praise be to God, who feeds the world with his goodness, grace and mercy." Then he added, "This is my blood, the blood of the New Covenant, which is poured out for men."

They each drank in turn from the cup that he handed them. He was giving his life for the people, he was pouring it out for them so that they could live new lives.

Nothing now would separate them from the love of God. Jesus had given them the New Testament.

Jesus Predicts His Betrayal

Jesus looked at the twelve men he had chosen to share his last supper on earth.

"Indeed, indeed, I tell you, tonight one of you will betray me," he said.

They were filled with horror. "Not *I*, Lord?" each one of them said. John, who was sitting on his right, said, "Lord, which one of us is it? Please tell us."

Jesus replied, "It is the one to whom I will give this piece of bread that I have dipped in the dish." He gave Judas Iscariot the bread and Judas exclaimed, "Surely you don't think *I* would betray you, Lord?" Jesus replied, "It is you who have said it."

The supper drew to its end. "I give you a new commandment," said Jesus. "Love one another as I have loved you. There is no greater love than this – that a man should lay down his life for his friends. You are my friends.

"When I have left you, I will send the Holy Spirit to take care of you. He will help you and guide you in everything that is true.

"Be prepared for people to hate you. But after darkness will come light, after sorrow, joy, and after grief, gladness.

"I am part of you and God is part of me. Now I pray to my Father that he will make us all one together."

Jesus Prays in the Garden of Gethsemane

"Come," said Jesus, "It is time to go." They walked through the sleeping city towards the Mount of Olives. When they reached the valley they heard the sound of water flowing over stones. It was the river Kedron. Jesus crossed the water. He turned to the disciples and said:

"This night you will all desert me. It has been prophesied, '*The shepherd, the companion of God, will be struck down and the sheep of his fold will be scattered.*' That hour has now come."

Peter cried, "Everyone else may desert you, but not I! I will give my life for you; I will suffer anything for you!"

Jesus said sadly, "Indeed, I tell you: this night, before the cock crows twice, you will disown me three times."

Peter cried, "No, never! Even if it means dying with you, I will never disown you!"

"Nor will I! Nor will I, Lord!" they all exclaimed.

They came to the garden of Gethsemane. It was surrounded by a wall, which had a gate in it. Jesus said to his disciples:

"Rest here while I go into the garden to pray."

He took with him into the garden Peter, James and John, who were the closest to him of all his disciples. Then he said to them:

"My soul is deeply troubled, and my heart is breaking. Stay here, and keep watch for me."

He seemed to be in terrible distress and misery as he moved away from them. He threw himself to the ground. With his face against the earth he prayed:

"*Abba* – Father, everything is possible for you. Do not, I beg you, make me drink this cup full of agony and death. Yet, I know it is not my will, but yours, that must be done."

The disciples wanted to go to him in his distress, but he had told them to stay behind. They watched him and waited, but their eyes were heavy with sleep.

When Jesus returned, his disciples were all asleep. He woke them and said to Peter:

"Simon, can you not keep watch for me for one hour? Your spirit is willing, but your body is weak. Watch and pray that you do not fall into temptation."

Again Jesus left them and went deeper into the garden. Again he sank to the ground and bowed low before God. His agony grew in him as he prayed, until the sweat poured from him into the earth like drops of blood.

He returned to his disciples. In their grief and tiredness they had fallen asleep once more.

For the third time he fell to the earth and prayed.

"Your will be done, Lord," he said.

Then he rose and came back to the disciples yet again. "Are you still sleeping?" he said to them. "Look! My betrayers have come!"

The Betrayal

"COME," Judas had said to the Temple police, "And I will take you to Jesus. The man I kiss will be Jesus himself. Seize him!"

They came through the garden gate, carrying torches and lanterns, swords and sticks.

Judas went up to Jesus. "Greetings, Master!" he cried, and kissed him.

Jesus replied, "Judas, my friend, why are you here? Do you betray the Son of Man with a kiss?"

The men drew their swords and closed in on Jesus. Peter barred the way; he struck at the high priest's servant and cut off his ear.

"Put back your sword in its sheath," Jesus said to him. "He who lives by the sword dies by the sword." He turned to the servant and touched his ear, and it was healed. Then he said to the men:

"Who are you looking for?"

"For Jesus of Nazareth," they replied. He said to them, "I am he."

The Temple police came forward. They bound his hands behind him with a rope, pulled off his headcloth and tore at his clothes.

Jesus said to the captain, "I am no criminal. You had no need to come for me in the night, armed with swords. Besides, you can see me every day teaching in the Temple. Why don't you arrest me there? Is it because you are afraid? Yes, this is the right time for you—the hour when everything is dark."

He looked around him. The disciples had run away and deserted him. He was alone with his enemies.

Peter Disowns Jesus

WHEN Jesus was taken prisoner, Peter followed him at a distance. He kept well back from the Temple guards and the soldiers, because he did not want them to see him and arrest him too.

They led Jesus to the palace of Caiaphas. Peter came into the courtyard and drew near to the fire that the guards had lit. He hoped to catch a word or two about what they would do to Jesus.

One of the maids who served in the palace came past. She looked curiously at Peter and then stopped.

"Weren't you one of his men?" she asked suspiciously.

"No, never!" exclaimed Peter.

He got up. The girl shrugged her shoulders and turned away. Peter hid himself in a dark corner of the yard. The voices died down again and there was silence.

In the distance a cock crowed.

Peter began walking towards the palace gate. He was anxious to escape before anyone else recognized him.

He reached the gate. The soldier standing guard there was talking to a servant girl and Peter tried to slip past them both without being seen. But the light of the guard's torch fell on his face, and the girl called out:

"You're one of them! You were with Jesus of Nazareth, and now you're running away!"

"No, no, no!" Peter exclaimed. "I don't even know the man! And I'm not running away!"

"Of course you are," said the guard. "You even speak the same dialect as he does. You're from Galilee!"

"I swear to you I don't know Jesus!" Peter shouted. He pushed past them through the gate and ran down the hill towards the dark city.

Suddenly he stood still. He could hear nothing but the pounding of his own heart.

In the distance a cock crowed again.

Then Peter remembered Jesus saying to him only a few hours before:

"Before the cock crows twice, you will disown me three times."

And he wept bitterly.

The Trial and the Mockery

AT LAST Jesus was in his enemies' hands. He was brought before the Jewish High Court of Justice, the Sanhedrin. Its members took their places in a semicircle and began questioning him. They called one witness after another, trying to find some evidence which would justify them in condemning Jesus to death. There were plenty of witnesses, but their evidence was all false. Finally two men came forward to say that Jesus had blasphemed against God. "He said that he could pull down God's holy Temple and build it up again in three days if he wanted to," one of them insisted.

Caiaphas looked at Jesus. He said in a loud voice, "I charge you to tell us whether you are the Messiah, the Son of the Living God."

Jesus answered, "I am he, and you shall see the Son of Man sitting on the right hand of the Almighty Power."

Then Caiaphas tore his cloak, as if to show that Jesus' words, like the torn cloth, could never be changed. He said:

"What need have we of further evidence? You have heard the blasphemy with your own ears. What is your verdict?"

The members of the Sanhedrin stood up. One after another they said: "He must be put to death." Then they too tore their cloaks from side to side.

Jesus was taken away. The guards beat him with their fists, and hit him in the face.

They spat on him, and then threw a cloth over his head so that he could not see and struck him again.

"Now prophesy," they jeered, "who was it who hit you?"

The Sanhedrin had no power to condemn Jesus to death; only the Roman governor, Pontius Pilate, could do that. So they led him to the governor's palace.

"What is this man accused of?" asked Pilate.

"He leads people astray and forbids us to pay taxes to Caesar. He also claims that he is the Messiah, the king of the Jews."

Pilate looked at Jesus. His clothes were torn and shabby. He certainly didn't look like a king.

"Are you the king of the Jews?" he asked.

"It is you who have said it," replied Jesus.

"This man is no criminal," said Pilate. "Why should I punish him on your flimsy evidence?"

He added, "Anyway, he's from Galilee. That is King Herod's province. Let Herod judge him."

So Jesus was taken to Herod. The king asked him many questions, but Jesus would not answer them. The priests and scholars of the Sanhedrin stood around Herod, trying to persuade him that Jesus was dangerous, that he was a political leader who threatened the power of Rome. Herod looked at Jesus. He was disappointed with him for not letting even one little miracle happen before his eyes. He waved the members of the Sanhedrin away.

"Take him back to Pilate!" he said. "I don't want to condemn him!"

Herod's soldiers began to jeer. They dressed Jesus in fine clothes, like those of a king in the circus, and led him around the courtyard, making fun of him.

The Crucifixion

JESUS was brought before Pilate once more. The Roman governor summoned the chief priests and leaders of the Jews before him and said:

"I cannot see why Jesus should be put to death. If you like, I can have him beaten, and then release him."

But the crowd that had gathered outside was gripped in a kind of fever. The people began to yell:

"Away with him! Free Barabbas instead!" They knew that Barabbas was a thief and a murderer, but they preferred him to Jesus. So Barabbas was freed. But the crowd still wanted Jesus to die. They howled:

"Crucify him! Crucify him!"

Pilate was afraid of this mad and evil mob, and tried to shout them down. When they took no notice of him, he called for a basin of water and washed his hands in front of them, so that they could see, even if they wouldn't hear, what he meant.

"I will have nothing more to do with you all. I wash my hands of your affairs. From now on you yourselves are responsible for what happens to Jesus of Nazareth!"

The Roman soldiers led Jesus away and beat him. When he was half dead they put a red robe on him, plaited a crown of thorns and pressed it down on his head. They put a reed in his right hand as a sceptre. "Look at the king of the Jews!" they laughed.

Pilate led Jesus out so that everyone could see him. He called in Latin, "*Ecce Homo—* behold the man! Here is your king!"

Jesus was taken out of the city. He was made to carry the cross on which he would be crucified. On it someone had written in Greek, Latin and Hebrew:

"Jesus of Nazareth, King of the Jews."

He was by now so weak that he fell several times as he carried the cross. Then the Romans made another man who was standing in the crowd, Simon of Cyrene, carry it for him.

People lined the roadside as the procession climbed up the stony hill to a place that was called Golgotha, which means "place of a skull," because it was the ground where criminals were executed. There a woman came forward, bringing Jesus a cup of wine mixed with myrrh to deaden his pain, but he did not take it.

The soldiers nailed him to the cross with a nail through each hand and through his feet. As they hammered the nails in, he said, "Father, forgive them, for they do not know what they are doing."

Then they set the cross up on end so that Jesus' weight hung from his pierced hands and feet.

The soldiers shared out Jesus' clothes between them, and cast the dice to decide who should take his robe.

John, his disciple, stood close by with a couple of women, supporting Jesus' mother. Jesus said to him, "She is your mother now." To Mary he said, "He is your son."

Two convicted thieves were crucified too, and their crosses set up on either side of Jesus. Despite his pain, one of them jeered at Jesus. But the other said to Jesus, "Remember me when you come to your kingdom." Jesus replied, "Today you will be with me in heaven."

Some members of the Sanhedrin murmured, "If he really is the Messiah, he will save himself. Then we will believe."

Suddenly the wind rose in the east and the sun was darkened. The people fled in terror.

Jesus cried, "My God, my God, why have you deserted me?" He was repeating words from one of the songs King David had written long before, which continue:

"*Let those who seek the Lord, praise him, and be glad in their hearts for ever. I shall live for all time, and shall serve him!*"

The Roman soldiers who had crucified Jesus and the thieves had brought some wine to drink during the long time they would have to wait for the men to die. It was rough and sour, but it quenched the thirst.

Jesus murmured, "I am thirsty."

One of the soldiers soaked a sponge in the wine and stuck it on his spear so that Jesus could wet his dry lips.

Jesus sucked a little wine from the sponge. Then he fell back against the cross.

"It is finished!" he said.

He cried out with a loud voice, "Into your hands, Lord, I commit my spirit."

Then his body died on the cross.

The Burial

Jesus' body hung dead on the cross. Soon it would be taken down and thrown in the mass grave with all the criminals.

It was the night before the Sabbath. A man was hurrying through the streets of Jerusalem towards Pilate's office. It was Joseph of Arimathea, a rich and powerful Jew, a member of the Sanhedrin. He believed in Jesus. He was going to ask Pilate for his body, so that Jesus might have the dignity of a private grave.

"What, is he dead already?" asked Pilate, in surprise. To be crucified usually meant a painful, slow death that often lasted for days.

The crucified man would find that he could not breathe with his arms stretched out. So he would raise himself up on his feet, nailed to the cross. Like this the air would rush into his lungs for a few seconds, then he would sink down again because of the pain. In the end the soldiers supervising the crucifixion would usually break his knees so that he could not straighten them. Then he would die of suffocation.

"Is this true?" Pilate asked his soldiers.

"Yes, sir; he has been dead for some time," they replied. "While he hung on the cross, one of our men pierced his side with a spear, and blood and water rushed out. But he was dead already."

"Take the body then," Pilate said to Joseph, "The power that was in him has left him with his death."

So Joseph and Nicodemus, another friend of Jesus and a member of the Sanhedrin like Joseph, went together up to Golgotha where the crosses stood. They lifted Jesus' body down, and wrapped it in linen cloth.

Three women, who had watched Jesus die on the cross had brought jars filled with myrrh and the oil of aloes to embalm his body as was the custom at that time. They worked in a hurry to prepare Jesus' body for burial because it would soon be the Sabbath and no Jew could do any work on that day.

They took the body to the new tomb that Joseph had bought for himself. It was cut of the rock in a hillside. They placed the body in it, wrapped in its winding sheet of linen. Then they rolled a great stone across the opening and went away.

The priests and Pharisees went to Pilate and said:

"Sir, we have reason to believe that Jesus' disciples will try to steal the body from the tomb. They want to pretend to the world that the Messiah is risen from the dead. After all, he did say, 'After three days I shall rise again.' Will you therefore give the order to have the tomb closely guarded for the next three days?"

"Yes," said Pilate, "I will. Go and make the tomb as safe as you think necessary; I will send you a guard of soldiers to keep watch."

The priests left, and went to the place where Jesus was buried. They wedged the stone fast, and put a seal on it. Then they stationed a guard of soldiers around it.

[278]

The Resurrection

THE sun had set and the Sabbath was over. Mary Magdalen and two other women prepared oils to anoint the body of Jesus a second time, because it had been done so hurriedly and incompletely before. All of them were followers of Jesus and they wanted to show their respect and love for him by taking care of his body as carefully as they could.

It was dark, and no one saw the three women make their way quietly through the streets and out of the city. They walked up along a narrow path to the rock where Jesus lay buried.

The night was lifting; a light rose in the east. The women stood still, looking at the tomb. The stone was no longer in front of it. It had been rolled away.

They walked fearfully towards the dark mouth of the cave. They leaned in to see better. A young man was there, dressed in a bright, white robe. He said:

"Do not be afraid. Are you looking for Jesus who was crucified? He is not here." He pointed to the side of the tomb. "That is where they laid him. He is gone from here. Why do you look for the living among the dead? Remember that he told you while he was still in Galilee that he would rise again on the third day."

The women were overcome with terror. They ran back to the house where the rest of the disciples were staying and cried out to Peter:

"They have taken the Lord out of the tomb, and we do not know where he is."

Peter and John ran up to the tomb to see for themselves. John ran ahead, leaving Peter behind. He looked into the tomb. By now the sun had risen and its rays fell deep into the inside of the rock.

John saw the winding sheet lying there, but he was too awed to go in. Simon Peter came up. He ran past John, into the cave. The linen strips that had been wound around the body lay on one side, while the cloth that had covered his head lay on the other. They puzzled about what it could mean, and then they returned to the city.

Mary Magdalen had stayed near the tomb, weeping and mourning for Jesus. Then two angels appeared before her. "Woman, why are you crying?" they said to her.

"They have taken away my Lord and I do not know where he is!"

She looked around and saw a man standing nearby. "Woman, why are you crying?" he said.

Supposing that he must be the gardener, Mary answered:

"Sir, if you have taken him away, tell me, please, where he is, so that I can carry him away."

"Mary!" he said to her.

Mary looked at him. "*Rabboni!*" she cried, "Master!" For it was Jesus.

"You must not touch me now," he said. "I have not yet gone to my Father. Go and tell the others that I am going to my Father and your Father, to my God and your God."

The Disciples
See Jesus

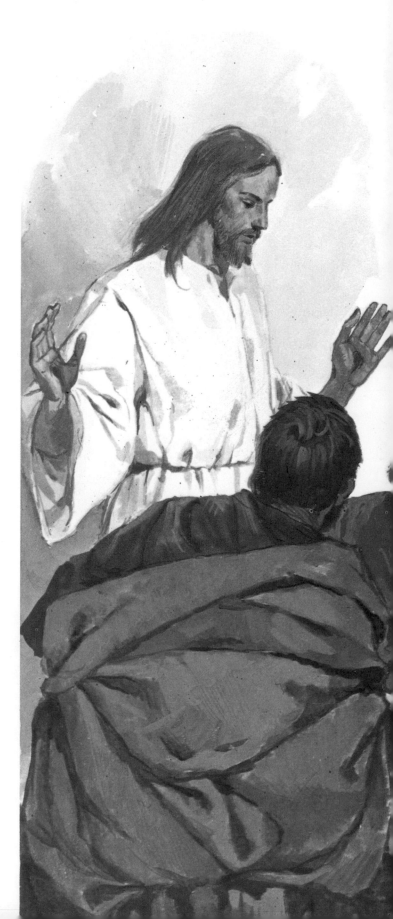

THAT same day two of the disciples left Jerusalem and went to the village of Emmaus. Their hearts were so full of what had happened that they could speak of nothing else.

While the two of them were deep in conversation Jesus himself came and walked along the road alongside them. They did not recognize him. He said:

"What are you talking about so seriously?"

They stopped, their faces full of misery. "You must be the only stranger in Jerusalem," they said, "who hasn't heard all the things that have happened there recently!"

"What things?" asked Jesus.

"Oh, about Jesus of Nazareth. How our priests and rulers have had him crucified . . . what's more, some of our women have been to the tomb and have seen angels there, who say he has risen from the dead."

Jesus said, "Do none of you understand that the Messiah must suffer all this so that the prophecies can be fulfilled?"

They reached Emmaus. The disciples said, "Stay with us, please. Darkness is falling. It will soon be night."

He sat down at the table with them, and took a loaf of bread. He gave thanks to God, broke it in pieces and gave the pieces to them. Then their eyes opened wide.

"It's Jesus!" they exclaimed. But before they could say any more Jesus had disappeared.

They hurried to Jerusalem to tell the others: "Jesus is risen! We have seen him!"

[282]

Thomas Doubts

THE apostles did not expect to see Jesus again once he was buried. They found it difficult to believe the men and women who said they had seen him.

"You only saw what you wanted to," they said. "You imagined everything!"

The men who had seen him at Emmaus insisted, "He broke bread with us, and we recognized him!"

Suddenly Jesus was there, in their midst. The doors were locked for fear of the Temple police. No man could have come through them.

"Peace be with you!" he said. "Why are you worried, and why do you doubt me? Look at the marks in my hands where the nails pierced them. Feel me; I am no ghost."

Thomas, one of the twelve, was not there that evening. When the others told him later, he would not believe them.

"Unless I see the marks of the nails in his hands and feet, I shan't believe it," he said.

A week later they all met again, and this time Thomas was with them.

Suddenly Jesus was standing in their midst.

"Peace be with you!" he said. Then he looked directly at Thomas. "Put your finger here, in the wounds in my hands and body. Then you will believe."

"My Lord and my God!" cried Thomas.

"You believe because you have seen me," Jesus said to him. "Happy are those who can believe even without seeing me."

Jesus at the Sea of Galilee

THE disciples went back to Galilee. They felt at home there, and they began once more to do the work they had been doing before Jesus called them.

One evening Simon Peter said, "I'm going fishing."

"We'll come with you," said the others. They were Thomas, Nathanael, James and John, and two others.

They dragged their nets across the lake all night, but caught nothing. Dawn rose and a new day began. Jesus appeared on the shore.

"Have you caught anything, friends?" he called. "No," they called back. They did not recognize him.

"Then throw the net on the right side of the boat," he said. "The fish lie there."

They lowered the net and it filled up immediately with fish. John, who had always been closest to Jesus, looked again at the figure on the shore. "It's the Lord!" he said.

They made for the land, Simon swimming the last 100 yards to get there quicker. Jesus had lit a charcoal fire on the beach.

"Bring me some fish," he said. They pulled the net ashore, and counted 153 fish in it.

Jesus gave them some bread and fish to eat. Then he said to Simon Peter:

"Simon, son of John, do you love me?"

"Yes, Lord," he replied, "You know that I do."

"Then feed my sheep," said Jesus. "Look after my people when I am gone."

The Ascent into Heaven

JESUS remained on earth for 40 days after his resurrection, showing himself to his disciples and to those who had loved him during his life on earth. There were some among them who still did not dare to believe that he had returned. Then, when they saw him with their own eyes, they fell on their knees and worshipped him.

He had done everything that the prophets in the Old Testament said he would. He had brought light into the world, and had won them back to God by dying for them on the cross. He had founded his kingdom. He had brought love and joy and peace into the world.

On the last day Jesus led his disciples to a hill outside Jerusalem. He raised his arms and blessed them. Then he said:

"All power on heaven and on earth has been given to me. You must go now, and call new disciples to follow you from all the nations of the earth, and baptize them in the name of the Father and of the Son and of the Holy Spirit. Teach them to do everything I have told you to do. And remember, I will always be with you, even to the end of the world."

As he said these words, a cloud came down from heaven and hid him from their sight. The cloud became a light, and the light filled the sky and the earth, and covered everything on the earth with glory.

The Beginning of the Church in Jerusalem

JESUS had said, "Stay in Jerusalem until God sends you power from on high."

The city was filled with pilgrims who had come for the feast of Pentecost. It was the day of thanksgiving for the wheat harvest and for the giving of the Law to Moses.

God chose this day to send his Spirit into his people, to found his Church, and give them his new law of love.

The disciples were all gathered together when suddenly there came from the sky a rushing noise like that of a great wind. It filled the house where they were staying. Tongues of fire appeared, which settled above the head of each of them. They were filled with the Holy Spirit, and began to speak in all the languages of the world about God and his love. People gathered in the street outside to ask what was going on.

Peter came out to them and said, "My friends, the prophecy has been fulfilled that says, '*God pours down his spirit on all people; young men shall see visions; old men shall dream dreams.*' So repent, and be baptized in the name of Jesus Christ, and then you can have your sins forgiven and receive the gift of God's Holy Spirit."

More and more people were baptized and joined in the fellowship of the Church. They met every day and broke bread together in their homes, and shared simple joys, constantly praying to God.

The Healing of the Lame Beggar

ONE afternoon Peter and John were on their way to the Temple to pray. At the Beautiful Gate they saw a beggar being carried along in the crowd. He had never been able to walk, and spent his days sitting at this gate, begging for money.

When he saw Peter and John coming towards him he stretched out his hand.

"Give me something!" he begged.

Peter stopped. "Look me in the eye!" he commanded. The man looked at him expectantly, hoping for a generous gift.

"I have no silver and gold," said Peter, "but what I have shall be yours. In the name of Jesus Christ of Nazareth, *stand up and walk!*" And he took him by the right hand and helped him up.

At once strength returned to the cripple's feet and ankles. He jumped to his feet and stood, and then walked forward. He went with Peter and John into the Temple, where he kept moving his limbs and stretching them, thanking God all the time.

"What is this?" said the people. "Isn't that the beggar who used to sit at the gate?"

They followed him around, pushing and jostling each other so much that the beggar clung to Peter and John in fear. Peter turned round. He said to the people:

"Why are you surprised? God has done this; through the power of Jesus Christ, his Son, he has healed this man."

[287]

The First Martyr

"THE Christians are always helping one another; the rich share their food with poor," the priests and elders were told by their spies. "They have appointed seven men whom they call deacons, to distribute the food. There's even a rabbi among them, called Stephen."

The Jewish leaders were frightened. People were paying less and less attention to the laws of Moses; the new gospel of Christ was beginning to infect Jews all over the country. "We must stamp it out by force!" they said. Then one day they heard Stephen preach, "You have murdered Jesus Christ, the Son of Man."

The people were furious. They shouted at him, and shook their fists. Stephen looked over their heads and said gently:

"I see the heavens opening and the Son of Man standing at the right hand of God."

The people rushed at him and knocked him down. Then they dragged him out of the city, and began to stone him to death.

A rabbi called Saul was standing in the crowd. He watched with satisfaction as the stones hit Stephen. He was a Jew who had been born at Tarsus in Asia Minor, and he was particularly anxious that this new religion should not push aside the older Jewish faith. He heard Stephen cry, "Lord, forgive them!" as the stones knocked him down. Then he called, "Lord Jesus, receive my spirit!" and died. Saul had witnessed the murder of the first Christian martyr.

The Conversion of Paul and His Escape

THE rabbi Saul became one of the bitterest enemies that Jesus' followers had. He was given authority by the high priests to arrest anyone who had broken the laws of Moses.

With the Temple police he searched the city, breaking into the houses where Christians met, and taking them prisoner. Men and women were cruelly beaten by Saul's command, and many of them fled from Judaea to form new communities around the Mediterranean coast.

Saul heard that the Jews in Damascus had begun praying to Christ. The *gospel*, or 'good news', as Christ's followers called his teaching, was spreading across the world like dawn across a night sky. Saul decided to go to Damascus and arrest these people himself.

Saul, later to be called Paul, was a stubborn man from a strict Jewish family, and he was a Roman citizen, an important privilege because, among other things, it gave him freedom to travel throughout the Roman empire. Saul was a fine scholar but, like all Jewish boys, he had also been taught a trade. He was a tentmaker. He was rich and powerful; above all, he longed to get rid of the influence of Christ and make the old Jewish religion live again.

He went to the high priest in Jerusalem. "These Christians are growing more powerful every day," he said. "I have heard a new group of them has formed in Damascus. They must be stamped out! Let me go there to attend to it myself!"

He persuaded the high priest to write to the heads of the synagogues in Damascus asking them to give Saul the names of any Jews there whom they knew, or suspected, to be Christians.

"I will have them arrested," Saul told the high priest, "and bring them back to Jerusalem."

He was riding along the caravan route to Damascus, accompanied by a troop of Temple police when suddenly there was a blinding flash of light. Saul fell to the ground and lay there quite still. A voice called out to him:

"Saul, Saul, why do you fight me?"

"Who are you, Lord?" cried Saul.

"I am Jesus, whom you are persecuting. I have chosen you to be my friend and helper. Stand up and go to Damascus. There you will be told what to do."

Saul raised himself from the ground. He had closed his eyes because of the blaze of light that had made him fall to the ground. Now he opened them again, but the light was still there—he could see nothing else. For three days he was blind; he ate and drank nothing, but kept praying to God. Then God sent a Christian named Ananias to Saul, to heal him.

"Saul, my brother," said Ananias, "The

Lord has sent me to give you back your sight, and to baptize you so that you will be born again in Christ."

He laid his hands on the blind man's head. It seemed to Saul that at his touch heavy shutters were lifted from his eyes. He could see again, and what he saw was sharp and beautiful because it was lit by the love of God.

From that hour on Saul became a follower of Christ. All the energy he had put into persecuting the Christians was turned instead to helping them. He spoke of love where before he had spoken of hate, and the crowds who flocked to hear him were not only Jews but Gentiles (the Jews' word for everyone who was not a Jew) too.

"There are men in the synagogues who want to murder you!" his friends warned him. "Day and night they are watching for you; every city gate is guarded so that you won't escape them. You must leave this city secretly."

One of the Christians in Damascus had a house beside the city wall, with a window that opened onto it. Saul was taken there at night. There was no moon and it was too dark for the night watchman in the tower to see beyond the nearest battlement.

A group of Christians waited in the shadows beneath the wall while others on the battlements lowered Saul slowly down inside a big basket tied to a rope. When it reached the ground, Saul's friends helped him climb clear of it. Then he turned southwards, towards Jerusalem, and began walking into the night.

When he arrived in Jerusalem he immediately went to the community of Christians there. They shut the door in his face. They could not believe that their enemy had become one of them.

Barnabas—his name means 'comforter'—was the first to trust Saul. "Come to us," he said, "and join the brotherhood of Christ."

The Teaching of Peter and His Escape

THERE was a man living in Caesarea whose name was Cornelius. He was a Roman soldier who lived an exceptionally good life and gave help to anyone who needed it, whether he was a Roman, an African, or a Jew. One day an angel came to him in a vision and said, "Cornelius!"

"What is it, Lord?" he asked in terror. The angel replied:

"Your heart is filled with God's light and he has seen your goodness from Heaven. Send three men to Joppa to a man called Simon Peter. He is staying in a house by the sea, with another Simon, a tanner. Tell him to come to you. The Lord needs him here."

The next day, while Cornelius' messengers were still on their way to the city, Peter went to the flat roof of the house in Joppa to pray. God sent him a vision—he saw an enormous sheet coming down from

the sky towards him. It was filled with every kind of animal, fish and bird. A voice said to him:

"If you are hungry, Peter, eat these creatures." Peter saw that there were pigs and hare among the animals, as well as fish and birds which the laws of Moses forbade every Jew to eat.

"Oh, no, Lord!" he said. "They are unclean!"

The voice said, "It is not for man to say which of God's creatures are clean or unclean, nor which of man's races are good or bad. Do not judge anything that God has made."

While Peter was still puzzling about the meaning of his vision the messengers sent by Cornelius arrived. They invited him back to their master's house.

Peter went with them, and as soon as Cornelius saw him he fell down on his knees in front of him.

"Don't worship me!" said Peter. "I am just an ordinary man like you!"

A large number of Cornelius' friends had gathered in the Roman's house. They were all Gentiles and Peter knew that by mixing with them and eating their food he was disobeying Jewish law. But now he understood the vision he had had on the roof top. God had told him that all creatures and all people are equally worthy in his eyes, and that we must not judge them or divide them into groups.

So Peter broke bread and drank wine with the Romans, and did it remembering that Christ had died to set all men free.

Soon afterwards Peter was arrested by King Herod Agrippa, who had succeeded Herod Antipas on the throne. But an angel came to him in prison and led him out, past sentries who did not see him and iron gates that opened to let him through.

Peter was free once again, to travel the world with his good news about Christ.

[293]

Paul's First Journey

Saul's life had become completely changed. He could not understand it all at once, and so he went off on his own for a while, into the deserts of Arabia. Like others before him—Moses, Elijah, Jesus—he needed to spend time away from other people, alone in a silent wilderness.

Before, when he was still a rabbi, he had wanted to judge what was good and evil in others. Now he realized that God accepts men just as they are, as a father accepts his child.

Saul returned to the people who needed him. He spent twelve years working quietly and simply among the poor and the sick. Then one day God called him. He was to go on a journey that would be a turning point in the story of Christianity. He was to travel to Antioch, an important city.

"A miracle has happened in Antioch. Jews and Gentiles are living together. They meet to pray and share the Lord's supper. They need you there, Saul, to tell them more about Christ," said Barnabas.

Saul stayed in Antioch for a whole year. He lived in danger all the time he was there, for the Jews of the synagogues hated him and would gladly have heard of his death. But Saul did not die; at Antioch he laid the foundations of Christ's Church, in which Christians from all nations of the world would come together in peace and love.

[294]

Once Saul went to Cyprus where the Roman governor of the island, whose name was Sergius Paulus, sent for him and asked him to preach about Jesus. But a Jewish sorcerer named Elymas called out, "Don't listen to him!" Saul knew that the Devil was speaking through him, and struck him blind. When the governor saw that Saul had such powers, he said, "I too believe in your God."

Later, when their work was going well, Saul and Barnabas set out to carry the gospel to Cyprus and to Attilia, to Lystra and to Derbe. They travelled mostly on foot, carrying water in a goatskin and a bag of bread, cheese and dried fruit. They walked along paved Roman roads and across sandy deserts. They slept on mountain slopes and on the edge of swamps. Saul wrote:

"We were in danger from rivers, in danger from bandits, in danger in the desert, in danger at sea, in danger among traitors. We suffered hunger and thirst, cold and sleeplessness. We were always oppressed but never crushed, often at a loss but not lost, we were hounded by men but never abandoned by God, and though our enemies beat us we were never destroyed."

Paul's Second Journey

FROM now on Saul used the name the Romans gave him – Paul. He returned to Jerusalem with Barnabas, and a meeting of members of the new Church was called to discuss a problem that was worrying some of them. "Do we expect the Gentiles to become Jews before they become Christians?" they asked. "Do they have to eat Jewish food? Do they have to be circumcized?"

Paul persuaded them that they did not; he told them that faith and love were more important than rules and traditions. Then Paul and Barnabas returned to Antioch and continued their teaching there and in other Mediterranean cities.

Paul wanted to travel to the east, as he had before, but a strange thing kept happening. Each time he set out, something stopped him. Then one evening he was in the port of Troas, talking to the seamen who had come there from Rome and Greece. With him were Silas and Timothy, and a Greek doctor called Luke. That night Paul had a dream. He was standing on the shore, as he had been doing that day, looking towards the distant lands of the west. The sun lay low over the mountains, the sea rose and fell around the islands. Suddenly he saw a man across the water. He stretched out his arms and called:

"Come, Paul, help us! Come here!"

Paul awoke. He told Luke what he had dreamed, and together they set sail. They arrived in Athens, and brought the word of Christ to a new continent – Europe.

Paul's Third Journey

IT was evening. Paul was on his third great tour. He had stopped off at Troas to speak to the Christian community there. The upstairs room was warm and filled with people, and the windows were open to the night. A boy named Eutychus sat perched on the window sill. Everyone in the room was listening to Paul, and none of them noticed that the boy had fallen asleep. Suddenly he pitched over the edge and fell three storeys to the stones below.

He seemed to be dead. But Paul bent down and gently lifted him in his arms.

"He lives," he said, and carried him into the house. The Christians stayed talking to Paul until daybreak, then they left, taking Eutychus with them, quite unharmed.

"If I speak with the voice of an angel," wrote Paul to the Christians at Corinth, "and feel no love, then my words are ugly and without music. If I speak like a prophet and know everything, and even have the power to move mountains, but have no love, I am nothing.

"If I give everything I have to the poor, and if I am willing to die for my faith, but have no love, it means nothing.

"Love is patient, love is kind, love is not envious. Love does not boast, nor is it proud. Love harms no one. Love is generous; it never holds a grudge. Love takes no pleasure in the weakness of others, but is joyful when it sees the truth.

"It endures everything, believes everything, hopes for everything, bears everything. Love never fails.

"We have faith, hope and love, but the greatest of these is love."

Paul in Jerusalem and Rome

PAUL wanted to go to Rome, the capital of the world. But before he set out, he had to return to Jerusalem. He had a feeling that this would be his last journey to the City of David. He wanted to say good-bye – "God be with you" – to his people there.

"Don't go back!" his friends warned him. "Your enemies want to kill you. You have upset too many Jews abroad!" But Paul replied:

"I belong to Israel. I must return. Did Jesus, our Master, flee from Jerusalem?"

He arrived in the city, bringing money for the poor. He went to the Temple to bathe, pray and offer sacrifices according to the Jewish law. When the crowd saw him they recognized him at once and hated him. Here was the man who had mixed Jews and Gentiles and had brought the words of Jesus to all nations. He had helped to split the Jewish faith in two.

"Kill him! Kill him!" they cried, but the Roman soldiers stopped them. They carried him on their shoulders, high above the howling mob, to the Roman captain of Jerusalem. He took Paul under his protection because he was a Roman citizen, and smuggled him out of the city.

Later Paul was imprisoned by the Romans in Caesarea and kept in prison for two years. During this time he dictated letter after letter to the growing Christian communities.

To the Christians at Philippi he wrote, "Enjoy yourselves in God. Be gentle with one another and always remember how close you are to God.

"Don't worry about anything. Tell God everything, big or small, that you are thinking about. The peace of God, which is greater than anything we know, will guard you and keep you in Christ."

To the Christians at Colossae he wrote:

"Christ is in you. Don't let anyone worry you by telling you what you ought to eat or drink, or on what days you must go to church. None of these things is important. The solid fact, the centre of everything, is Christ. And when you know that, you also know that there is no difference between Greek and Jew, stranger and friend, slave and free man, for Christ lives in them all."

Paul's last letter was written to a Christian landowner named Philemon, who lived in Laodicea in Asia Minor. Philemon had a slave named Onesimus, who had run away to Rome and was living in hiding there.

One day, Onesimus heard Paul speaking to some Roman Christians about Christ's teaching. "Is it possible for a slave like me to become a Christian?" he asked Paul, and Paul replied, "It is possible for *anyone* to become a Christian."

So Onesimus was baptized, and Paul sent him back to Philemon, his master, with a letter in which he had written:

"Do not punish Onesimus. He left you as a slave. He returns to you now as a brother Christian. Welcome him as you welcomed me, for we are all brothers in Christ."

Luke, the Greek doctor, and Matthew and Mark, too, had been busy writing down the stories and sayings of Jesus.

A new governor of Judaea was appointed, and he sent Paul to Rome, to be tried before Caesar. Luke went with Paul on the ship, and he tells us what happened next:

"Great clouds piled up in the north-east. The sails flapped in the wind. We lowered the mainsail and fastened the hatches, and let ourselves be driven by the storm. The ship was lifted on the backs of giant waves and then sucked into troughs of black water. It began to list to one side, and we threw some of the cargo overboard—sacks of grain and millstones.

"Paul cried above the howling of the storm, 'Have courage! None of you will die, only the ship will be destroyed. Last night an angel came to me from my God, and he said, Do not be afraid. You will reach Rome and God will preserve all those with you.'

"We saw neither sun nor stars for many days. We waited for the storm to drive us onto rocks; we were terrified. At last the ship hit a sand bank; it broke apart and the water rushed in. Those who could swim jumped overboard, others grasped at planks floating by, and in the end everyone was able to struggle ashore safely on the coast of the island of Malta.

"We lit a fire and Paul helped to stoke it with wood. An adder bit his arm, but he shook it free. Because he did not die, the people thought he was a god.

"After three months we set sail and reached Rome at last. There the Jewish leaders came to see Paul in prison, and he talked to them about Jesus. Some were converted, but others argued with him for hours. Finally Paul said, 'I will take God's message to the Gentiles—*they* will listen.'"

Paul's Last Years

WE do not know much about Paul's last years. He stayed in Rome, and continued to preach and to write. He remained fearless in the face of his enemies. He would say to his friends:

"What can separate me from the love of God? Can pain or hardship, cruelty, danger, or death? No, for we are able to conquer all such hardships through Christ's love for us. For I am certain that neither death nor life, nor angels nor powers, nor present nor future, nor natural forces nor height nor depth, nor anything that exists, can separate us from the love of God, which is shown us by Christ, our Lord."

"Don't owe anything to anyone," he wrote, "except the debt of loving one another. For the man who loves another has fulfilled the law of God. Wake up! Live! The night is nearly over, the day has almost dawned. Shake off the power of darkness and put on the armour of light. In everything let us remember we belong to Christ."

In the year A.D. 64 there was a terrible fire in Rome. The Emperor Nero cried, "The Jews have done this! They refuse to worship me as a god! Kill them!"

So the long persecution of Jews and Christians began.

Tradition says that Paul was killed at that time, along with many other Christians who died as martyrs, rather than give up their faith. The last words of his we know about are these:

"The Lord will bring me safely to his heavenly kingdom. Glory be to him for ever!"

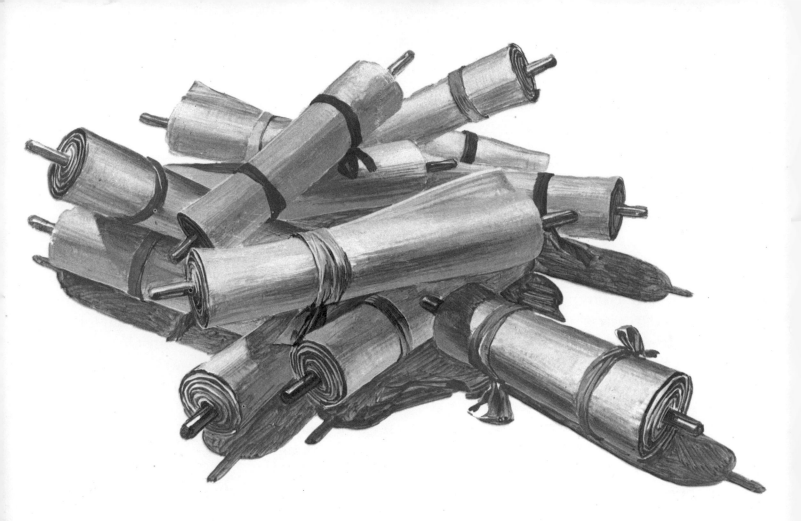

The Letters of Peter

IN the year A.D. 70 the city of Jerusalem was utterly destroyed. The old enmity between Jews and Romans had at last erupted into open war. The Jews were outnumbered, but they resisted the great armies of Rome so stubbornly that for a time it seemed as if they might win the war. In the end they were defeated. The Holy City fell after one of the greatest struggles in history. The Temple was destroyed and the city was burned to the ground.

The followers of Christ who made up the Christian Church were scattered in many places, and they kept in touch by writing letters to each other. The Roman Empire had no postal system, so the letters were carried from one community to the next by hand.

"I can speak," wrote Simon Peter from Rome, "as one who actually saw Christ suffer. He suffered for us, so that he could bring us to God. His body died, but his spirit remains alive. You are all responsible for one another. Live simply; prepare yourselves for the time when our Lord will come to earth again. Be humble, trust in God. Always watch out, for your enemy the Devil is always around, like a lion looking for his prey. Resist him; stand firm in your faith and remember that you are never alone in your pain. Your fellow Christians are suffering too. And when your brief earthly pain is over God will take you to him and heal you."

The Vision of John

THE last book in the Bible was written at a time of great suffering for the people who called themselves Christians. The old Roman world was seriously threatened by the young Church of Christ. The more the leaders in Rome tried to suppress the new faith, the more strongly it took root.

Among those who were imprisoned was a man called John. He was banished from the city of Ephesus in Asia Minor and taken to the island of Patmos, to be imprisoned there. Here he wrote the *Book of Revelation* to give courage to his fellow Christians throughout the world. The book is a poem about the struggle between the Church and the Roman Empire, in which finally Rome is destroyed and the world is changed into the holy city of God:

"And I saw a new heaven
And a new earth

For the first heaven
And the first earth
Had disappeared.
And I saw the Holy City
The new Jerusalem,
Coming down from heaven, from God,

Dressed like a bride for her husband.
And I heard a loud voice
Saying from the throne,
'See, God is with men,
And he will live with them,
And they will be his people.
And he will wipe away their tears,
And there will be no more death,
No more mourning, nor crying,
Nor will there be any more pain,
For these things have passed away.'

And he who was sitting on the throne of
    heaven said:
'See, I am making everything new.'
At the end heaven and earth
Will vanish too; there will be
Neither darkness nor death, for everything
Is changed into the light of God.
Men will see God,
And he will shine his light on them;
He is Alpha and Omega,
The beginning and the end."

The Journeys of St Paul

First Journey
Second Journey
Third Journey
Fourth Journey

Km 0   100   200   300
Miles 0   50   100   150

Italy

Rome

Puteoli

Macedonia

Philip

Berea   Thessalonica

Rhegium

SICILY

Corinth   Athens

Greece

Syracuse

MEDITERR

MALTA

Boundary of the Roman Empire

Cy

C